Michael Caduto's *Through a Naturalist's Eyes* is rich with fascinating details. It is sure to educate and entertain everyone, whether an avid naturalist or the casual observer. No matter what you may think you know, this book offers something new to discover about the natural world around us.

PAUL REZENDES author of *Tracking and the Art of Seeing* and *The Wild Within*

Reading Michael Caduto's book is like going for a walk and discovering something cool that you have never seen before—from rare mussels to the effects of cold on trees to geometric patterns to seaweeds. He uses his lifetime of experience in New England to create entertaining natural history stories on a wide range of topics from both common and rare species to the evolving history of the human relationship to nature. Michael successfully balances a discussion of threats to our unique landscape with positive actions that individuals can take both in their yards and in their communities.

KAREN LOMBARD director of stewardship, Massachusetts chapter, The Nature Conservancy

Nature is beautifully complex, and the closer you look the more you see of that beauty. Michael Caduto is an engaging explorer and observer who helps readers see and appreciate the world around us.

ANDREW FISK executive director, Connecticut River Watershed Council

If every walk you take—in the woods, up a stream, down city sidewalks, along a beach—gets you wondering about the natural world around you, spend some time with this book! Michael Caduto's well-researched, engaging essays are a combination of personal narrative, natural history, and bits of conversations—like a naturalist's dinner party with a roomful of ecologists, biologists, and storytellers: full of life and full of place. Adelaide Murphy Tyrol's illustrations beautifully illuminate each topic, highlighting the focal point and leaving room for the reader's own imagination. I read this book in one big gulp, but I'll return to it to savor passages again and again.

LISA PURCELL director, Four Winds Nature Institute, and co-editor, *Hands-On Nature*

T0341819

Caduto takes readers far afield on a tour of habitats through history. He blends science, humor, and lore to create a stunning narrative for young and old alike, with an intriguing dose of Native American culture. The effects of rapid climate change—scary scenarios—are never sugar-coated. Caduto recounts what New England scientists have observed: what we know and that which remains uncertain. He gently and consistently reminds us that "our own well-being is closely intertwined with the fare of the natural world."

DAVE ANDERSON  director of education, Society for the Protection of New Hampshire Forests, and co-host of NHPR's *Something Wild*

# THROUGH A
# NATURALIST'S EYES

Michael J. Caduto

ILLUSTRATED BY ADELAIDE MURPHY TYROL

EXPLORING THE NATURE

OF NEW ENGLAND

# Through a
# Naturalist's Eyes

University Press of New England
Hanover and London

University Press of New England

An imprint of Brandeis University Press

Text © 2016 Michael J. Caduto

Illustrations © 2016 Adelaide Murphy Tyrol

All rights reserved

Printed and bound by CPI Group (UK) Ltd, Croydon, CR0 4YY

Designed by Mindy Basinger Hill

Typeset in Adobe Jenson Pro

For permission to reproduce any of the material in this book, contact
Brandeis University Press, 415 South Street, Waltham, MA 02453,
or visit brandeisuniversitypress.com

Library of Congress Cataloging-in-Publication Data

NAMES: Caduto, Michael J., author.

TITLE: Through a naturalist's eyes : exploring the nature of New England /
    Michael J. Caduto; illustrated by Adelaide Murphy Tyrol.

DESCRIPTION: Hanover : University Press of New England, 2016. |
    Includes index.

IDENTIFIERS: LCCN 2016018377 (print) | LCCN 2016039682 (ebook) |
    ISBN 9781611689891 (pbk.) | ISBN 9781512600131 (epub, mobi & pdf)

SUBJECTS: LCSH: Natural history—New England. | Phenology—
    New England.

CLASSIFICATION: LCC QH104.5.N4 C33 2016 (print) | LCC QH104.5.N4
    (ebook) | DDC 578.4/2—dc23

LC record available at https://lccn.loc.gov/2016018377

FOR ESTHER AND RALPH
*Source and touchstone*

FOR LINDA, NANCY AND MARY
*Hearts of my heart*

# Contents

STEWARDSHIP

# Acknowledgments

FIRST, AND MOST SINCERELY, to my wife, Marie Levesque Caduto, and to my other family and friends who lent their wholehearted support and endured the many ways in which I was absent while immersed in this manuscript. Thank you all for your understanding of the writing life.

To Adelaide Murphy Tyrol, for creating the inspiring cover image and the rich and diverse interior illustrations that animate the words and bring readers face to face with the many plants, animals, and landscapes that they encounter herein.

And to the many colleagues whose time and energy made this book possible. Every book is a collaborative effort born of the ideas, support, and generosity of a small creative community. My gratitude to the talented and dedicated staff at the University Press of New England who brought this book to life and sent it out into the world: Dr. Phyllis Deutsch, editor-in-chief; Michael Burton, director; Peter Fong, production editor; Sherri Strickland, sales manager; Rick Henning, director of marketing and sales; Barbara Briggs, publicist; and Thomas Haushalter, marketing manager. A special appreciation to the designer, Mindy Basinger Hill, for creating the pleasing book you hold in your hands. Having worked with some of the staff for over twenty-five years, my appreciation continues to grow for the role that UPNE plays in introducing popular, literary, and scholarly books to readers.

Most of the essays in this present book are adapted and expanded from columns I originally wrote for the popular syndicated newspaper series "The Outside Story," which is assigned and edited by *Northern Woodlands* magazine (northernwoodlands.org) and sponsored by the Wellborn Ecology Fund of New Hampshire Charitable Foundation (nhcf.org). I can't say enough about the patience and generosity of the excellent Outside Story editors with whom I've worked since 2002, including Virginia Barlow, Dave Mance III, Meghan Olliver, Elise Tillinghast, Chuck Wooster, and Dirk Van Susteren.

As a nature writer, I've also been fortunate to work with the editors at Mass-Audubon for the past fifteen years, writing regularly for *Sanctuary Magazine*. I've grown as a writer while enjoying many wonderful creative experiences collaborating with the staff, including John Hanson Mitchell (editor), Ann Prince (associate editor), and Rose M. Murphy (production editor).

Reviewers who read and comment on a manuscript are a critical part of any project of this magnitude. My heartfelt thanks to the major reviewers of this manuscript: Dr. Walter Ellison, lecturer on biology at Washington College in Chestertown, Maryland; and Marie Levesque Caduto, watershed coordinator for the Vermont Agency of Natural Resources.

Many experts in their respective fields gave generously of their time to review individual chapters, including Chris Bernier, Furbearer Project leader, Vermont Fish and Wildlife Department; Dr. Michael Blust, professor of biology, emeritus, Green Mountain College; Dr. Donald Cheney, associate professor, emeritus, Marine Science Center, Northeastern University; Mark Ferguson, zoologist, Natural Heritage Inventory, Vermont Department of Fish and Wildlife; Alan C. Graham, Vermont state entomologist; Blair Nikula, co-author, *Stokes' Beginner's Guide to Dragonflies and Damselflies*; Amy Singler, American Rivers; Rebecca Suomala, senior biologist, New Hampshire Audubon; and Harry S. Vogel, senior biologist and executive director, Loon Preservation Committee in Moultonborough, New Hampshire.

Charles H. Ashton, of Ashton Indexing, created a comprehensive reference—a map of literary tracks and signs—to help the reader locate the subjects and names that weave through the pages of this book.

And finally, to you, the reader, who completes the circle by bringing this book to life in your imagination.

# THROUGH A
# NATURALIST'S EYES

# Introduction

NEW ENGLAND IS A LAND that dwells in the heart of its people with a passion unequaled. It is also a region whose name was inspired more than five centuries ago by a place of rolling fields and farms that most of New England's current denizens have never seen firsthand. These hills and rivers, mountains and lakes, hold fast to a gentle beauty that captivates visitors from around the world, from places that possess a different appeal—beautiful in their own right—but an allure that rarely surpasses that of the Northeast.

For native and visitor alike, it is easy to become drawn into the grand sweep of the land; to see New England as an artist might envision the pieces of a folksy quilt, with widely varied swatches woven together to create a pleasing whole. But this is a living tapestry of complex bioregions and natural communities whose compositions of plants and animals have evolved over time, and whose boundaries shade into one another in a dynamic response to interactions with neighboring populations, the prevailing conditions of water, soil, topography, and a rapidly shifting climate.

As appealing as the ideal of New England is, ours is a real environment, inhabited by people and natural populations that vie for an ever-shrinking supply of space and resources. Forests are cut for fuel while farmland succumbs to roads, housing subdivisions, shopping plazas, and other developments. Our constant search for energy, and ways to transport it, cuts wide swaths through the landscape to deliver power from ever more remote locations.

Still, New Englanders are devoted to their home region and each year millions of visitors make a veritable pilgrimage to see the villages, cities, and countryside that have captured their imaginations. This book takes the reader on a journey to explore some of the plants, animals, natural places, and environmental issues of New England—from dragonflies, cuckoos and chipmunks to circumpolar constellations, phenology, and climate change. But please don't stop here; turn your literary foray into a real adventure into the natural world. Experience for yourself this fascinating place we call New England.

# *Prologue*

## CHIPMUNK CPR

I REMEMBER TWO THINGS BEST about the summer of 1980. After Mount St. Helens erupted and spewed her blanket of ash into the upper atmosphere, we experienced a brief spell of global cooling. At the time I was senior instructor at the Living Rivers Program—a summer environmental education camp in northern New Brunswick that was run by the Quebec-Labrador Foundation (QLF). Even to a native New Englander who had become accustomed to the impetuous weather of the North Country, the New Brunswick summer was not exactly balmy. As the volcanic haze spread eastward, it reduced the amount of sunlight reaching the ground. We had four frosts that year during the months of July and August. The swimming dock was quiet and subdued.

Most of all, I recall an event that I've retold many times since that frigid summer. It's one of the most remarkable experiences I have had in four decades of teaching about the natural world.

Our camp, which was run by QLF's Atlantic Center for the Environment, consisted of a rustic converted hunting lodge that was situated twelve miles up the Tabusintac River. There were no roads into the camp, which was surrounded by a vast expanse of spruce and fir forest with its wet, mossy ground cover. The only access was by the johnboats that made their weekly trip upriver to bring fresh food, other supplies, and children.

During the first session I worked with fifth- and sixth-graders: an enthusiastic, motley crew of kids; the sons and daughters of farmers and smelt fishermen who were mostly of Scottish and Micmac Indian descent. To begin our garden project, we dug into the only dry spot we could find in the thin, sandy soil that had been excavated to build the cabin. Here we planted a few rows of vegetable seeds with the hope that something would actually grow in the spare, acid earth. Having no fence to keep out the local plant-eating critters, I borrowed an old piece of a smelt fishing net from Clive Wishart, a local farmer and fisherman, and the camp proprietor. Clive was, both figuratively and literally, the salt of the Earth. I fashioned four wooden corner posts with my axe, strung the old smelt net around the garden, then buried its bottom edge.

Two days later, as I sat in the cabin working with some campers on their projects, a group of children ran in screaming, "Quick, hurry, there's a chipmunk caught in the net and it's stopped breathing!" The boys looked helpless and some of the girls were crying.

I dropped the pair of scissors I was holding, ran outside, and saw the unfortunate chipmunk, limp and lifeless, hanging with its neck twisted in the smelt net. It had tried to enter the garden, found the hole in the net too small, and become stuck with its head in and body out. In an attempt to free itself, the chipmunk had jumped repeatedly, winding the net around its neck like a noose.

"Do something!" the children screamed.

After struggling in vain to untangle the chipmunk, I ran back to the cabin, grabbed the scissors, and carefully cut the strands from around its neck.

"Do something to save it!" the children pleaded.

Whatever possessed me to try what I did next, I'll never know. Imagining how quickly I had seen a chipmunk's chest expand and contract as it breathed, I cradled the animal in my left hand and administered CPR chest compressions with my right index and middle fingers. During the minutes that followed, the entire camp crowded around to watch in a collective breath-holding of its own.

For a while, the exercise seemed hopeless. Each time I stopped my compressions, we could see that the chipmunk was still not breathing.

Then, to my complete surprise and amazement, I felt the tiny chest heave— once . . . twice . . . and again. I stopped the compressions. We all watched as that small ground squirrel began to take single breaths, with extremely long intervals in between.

Gradually, the breaths came quicker, but it was still lying on its side with eyes closed. When the pace of breathing seemed almost normal, the chipmunk suddenly sat up, looked at me in sheer terror, then bolted from my hand and ran off into the forest.

A cheer rang out over the chilly Tabusintac River. Everyone was screaming and hugging and jumping up and down.

And yes, as those who attend my storytelling programs often ask, this *is* a true story.

ANIMALS

# Mouse or Mole, Shrew or Vole?

PETRUCHIO'S PURSUIT, the bane of Padua, had a bark that cowered the meek, and a bite to match. Katherine the Shrew delivered her barbed wit with a rapier tongue.

"If I be waspish," she forewarned, "best beware my sting."

But Petruchio's charms, and persistent parries, countered Katherine's thrusts until, by the end of her tale, she was bereft of both bark and bite.

The famous shrew of Shakespeare's realm has nothing over the one that wanders our woodlands and fields. Among the most common mammals of New England, the northern short-tailed shrew tunnels below the radar of all but the most ardent naturalist. And although its shrill voice can reach above the range of human hearing, the bite of this mouse-sized marvel would put Petruchio's passion to shame, for it delivers a poison that can paralyze and kill its prey.

Our tale of the short-tailed begins with its name: *Blarina brevicauda*, where *brevicauda* is Latin for "short tail." If I had been a naturalist in Old England, I would have become wealthy if I'd had a twopence for every time a horse's hooves stirred the dust at my door and the rider dismounted with a flourish, bearing the familiar query: "Master of this house, I would beseech thee, what manner of creature is this that my feline has dropped with felicity at my own stoop, be it neither mouse nor mole, but something of the two?"

Mouse or mole, shrew or vole—when it comes to nature, we tend to stuff things we don't know into pigeonholes that are already defined by the familiar. If someone tells me their cat has left a present of a dead mouse on the doorstep, I ask the usual questions: How big is it? What color is the fur? How long is its tail? What size are the eyes and ears? How pointed is its nose? Because chances are that it's not really a mouse.

Here in New England, the deceased is often a 4- to 5-inch-long northern short-tailed shrew, with its dark gray fur, inch-long tail, pinpoint eyes, sharp nose, fur-covered ears, and stubby legs bearing sharp claws for digging. And the cat is not necessarily leaving the shrew as a gift: short-taileds have glands on the hips and belly that emit such a strong, musky odor that most predators can't stomach the idea of eating one. Snakes and owls actually will partake of the pungent, as will other shrews, which have a poor olfactory sense.

With a rate of metabolism that is sixty times that of a human, shrews are more often the predator than the prey. Wielding sharp teeth, short-tailed shrews can consume more than their own weight each day. They are not fussy about who or what they eat; insects, worms, and spiders are fair game, as are centipedes and salamanders. Meadow voles are a popular item on the menu, along with mice, snakes, small rabbits, eggs, the hatchlings of ground-nesting birds, and even other shrews.

Short-tailed shrews are particularly effective predators for their size be- cause they possess a weapon that is found among just a handful of mammals in existence—a poisonous bite. The toxin, which flows up along the lower incisors and into the wound caused by the bite, is similar to the venom of cobras and coral snakes. It immobilizes prey and causes respiratory failure in small mammals.

As if poison didn't lend enough of an advantage, tunneling short-tailed shrews navigate like bats and dolphins: they emit ultrasonic clicks that reflect back to their ears to create an aural picture of the surroundings. From as far as two feet away, a short-tailed shrew's echolocation helps it to find solid objects, holes, and places where grass may block a runway. Their sixth sense may even serve to identify predators and prey.

When the north wind blows, the short-tailed shrew's short summer coat grows longer and turns a darker shade of gray, making it appear very mole- like. But moles are larger and more robust insectivores with powerful front shoulders and outsized front feet and claws. The star-nosed mole has a 3-inch- long tail and an unmistakable sunburst-shaped nose bearing twenty-two pink rays that encircle the tip. Another species of local mole, the hairy-tailed mole, is about 6 inches long. They have a short, furry tail and their backs are

DEER MOUSE

MEADOW VOLE

HAIRY·TAILED MOLE

SHORT·TAILED SHREW

covered with fur that ranges from dark gray to black. In contrast, the rotund eastern mole has a sharp nose and naked tail. Each day, one of these feisty, 2- to 3-ounce critters can eat more than its own weight in earthworms, snails, millipedes, slugs, and insects. Their winter tunnels lie 10 to 20 inches beneath the surface.

The short-tailed shrew most closely resembles yet another species, the meadow vole, but voles are tawny brown in summer, turn grayer in winter, have a blunt nose and a tail that ranges from 1¼ to 2½ inches long. They have beady black eyes, short, rounded ears and chunky bodies that measure 6 to 7½ inches with the tail. Voles tunnel below the surface and create runways in the thick grass. Their food includes grass, seeds, grains, and tubers. Mice are blamed for much of the damage done by voles, which eat prodigious amounts of roots and countless flower bulbs, and are so fond of bark that they often girdle and kill young shrubs and trees. And meadow voles can produce up to seventeen litters each year!

When you look carefully at short-tailed shrews, moles, and voles, none resemble mice, which have large, prominent eyes, big ears, and tails about as long as their bodies. Our two common species, the white-footed mouse and the deer mouse, look very much alike. White-footed mice are reddish brown, with a dark patch running along the back. Deer mice have brownish-gray fur and are nearly 7 to 8½ inches long, including the 3- to 4-inch-long tail. Mice eat as much as a third of their weight in food each day, including lots of seeds, grains, nuts, and fruits. A third or more of their diet consists of animal foods such as small insects, grubs, and worms. They cache sizeable stores of food as autumn days grow shorter.

When a wintering "mouse" appears in one of the live traps I set in our porous, Civil War–era house, I look closely. Shrew? (Sharp nose, short legs and tail.) Mole? (Big shoulders, claws, and a longer tail.) Vole? (Brown, big, blunt nose.) Mouse? (Big ears and eyes, very long tail.) I handle them carefully on our journey of at least two miles, the minimum distance from which they won't later return. And I am especially careful when moving a shrew so as to avoid its painful, toxic bite.

# *Catamount*

## THE GAME IS AFOOT

MORE THAN SEVENTY-FIVE YEARS have passed since a mountain lion was hunted and killed in New England. In 1938 a Quebec trapper caught the last one on record—in Maine. New Hampshire's last killing occurred in the White Mountains in 1885. Alexander Cromwell shot the final and largest specimen ever recorded in Vermont in Barnard in 1881. It weighed 182 pounds and measured 7 feet long. A mount of this magnificent animal, along with Cromwell's rifle, is displayed at the Vermont Historical Society in Montpelier.

The mountain lion—aka cougar, puma, panther, or catamount (cat of the mountain)—has long occupied a mythic role in New England. In his 1853 book, *Natural History of Vermont*, renowned naturalist Zadock Thompson mentioned the strength and leaping ability of the mountain lion. "One of these animals took a large calf out of a pen in Bennington, where the fence was four feet high, and carried it off on his back," he wrote. "With this load, he ascended a ledge of rocks, where one of the leaps was 15 feet in height."

In the mid-1800s, mountain lions were considered such a threat to human life and livestock that the Vermont Legislature issued a bounty of $20 for each pelt. Adjusted for inflation, that would have equaled about $550 in today's dollars. The bounty—and the taming of the wilds—have had an impact, for in the East the mountain lion as a species has virtually disappeared.

Nonetheless, residents of northern New England seem to be on the lookout for them. Wildlife biologists in the region get plenty of reports of sightings, but most reports are cases of mistaken identity—people most likely are seeing bobcats, lynx, coyotes, or captive mountain lions that have escaped their en-

*Mountain lion or catamount.*

closures. Time and again, biologists play Sherlock Holmes, taking testimony from those reporting sightings and combing the outdoors for tracks, fur, and scat. They wield forensic tools worthy of a contemporary CSI drama—detailed lab exams of suspect droppings and DNA analysis of purported catamount fur.

Mountain lions are noticeably bigger than the other large mammals for which they are sometimes mistaken. A mountain lion can weigh well over 150 pounds and measure up to 8 feet long (tip of nose to end of tail), while a bobcat might weigh up to 35 pounds and reach 45 inches, a coyote 50 pounds and 53 inches, or a lynx 35 pounds and 40 inches.

Wild populations of mountain lions survive in southern Florida and in the mountains of the West. They make dens in caves and crevices, amid boulder outcroppings, and in dense underbrush. They range as far as 30 miles from their dens and eat as much as 12 pounds of prey per day—from rabbit to deer.

With western populations increasing, wildlife biologists conjecture that individual lions may be dispersing eastward. Catamounts have been spotted in New Brunswick, Ontario, and Nova Scotia, and in a few parts of New England, but a confirmed sighting does not necessarily mean that the animal has taken up residence. On June 11, 2011, a mountain lion was hit and killed by an SUV in Milford, Connecticut, along the Wilbur Cross Parkway. Its

DNA matched that of a male that had previously been trapped and studied in South Dakota, more than 1,500 miles away.

Douglas Blodgett, a wildlife biologist with the Vermont Fish and Wildlife Department, says "40 to 50 sightings" of catamounts are reported in Vermont each year. "But we still don't have tangible, solid evidence, such as scat, prey caches or dead mountain lions. There is no evidence of a viable catamount population in Vermont."

Blodgett, however, keeps an open mind. "On occasion, some of the sightings are very credible," he says. "These sightings could be explained by the exotic pet trade, which is ubiquitous in the United States. It's not beyond belief that some of these animals could have been purchased and escaped."

Still, a mature mountain lion and two cubs apparently were sighted in Craftsbury, Vermont, during the winter of 1993–94. Their scat contained fur that fish and wildlife officials determined, through microscopic analysis, to be that of a catamount.

"There is no definitive proof of mountain lions in New Hampshire (either)," says Mark Ellingwood, a wildlife biologist with that state's fish and game department. "DNA analysis of scat and hair samples have all been negative . . . mostly bobcats," he says. "Video evidence has pointed to being, not mountain lions, but bobcats, coyotes and feral cats."

Sounding like a detective, Ellingwood says: "We look for patterns in the evidence and look forward to receiving any evidence, particularly physical evidence. I have spoken to some very knowledgeable and very competent people who say they've seen mountain lions."

Maine's Department of Inland Fisheries and Wildlife reports tracks, droppings, and fur from catamounts in that state and neighboring New Brunswick. In 1997, Massachusetts biologists found scat near the Quabbin Reservoir. DNA analysis proved it was from a mountain lion, but some officials suspect it was a captive animal that had escaped.

So the search continues. If Sherlock Holmes were sleuthing the mountain lion today, he might doggedly turn to his sidekick and say, "Come Watson, come! The game is a . . . paw."

# The Swifts of Summer

DARTING THROUGH THE AIR while twittering in constant conversation, chimney swifts are a cheering presence over many cities and towns. True to their name, which comes from the Old English *swifan*—"to move in a course, sweep or revolve"—these loquacious birds etch great circles overhead, emerging at daybreak and continuing until they flutter down the chimney at dusk.

But swifts didn't always roost and nest in chimneys. Hollow trees, caves, and cliff faces were their natural habitat, especially trees in which the inside had rotted away following a lightning strike. In 1840 John James Audubon reported a communal roost of roughly nine thousand swifts living in a hollow sycamore tree. The first record of swifts nesting in chimneys dates to 1672, but swifts continued nesting in trees as well.

Few species have become so completely dependent on human-made structures for their existence. Laura Erickson, science editor at the Cornell Lab of Ornithology, says, "Chimney swift populations increased dramatically with the arrival of European settlers and the construction of chimneys. Brick chimneys are ideal for swifts to perch in."

Being one of just four species of North American swifts, our native chimney swift is a soot-colored bird that breeds east of the Rocky Mountains in the United States and southern Canada. Flying by daylight—their 5-inch bodies carried aloft on strong, stiff wings that span 12 inches—chimney swifts migrate northward in spring after wintering in northwestern and north-central South America.

Swifts return when insects emerge en masse in late April. Rapacious predators that can consume one-third of their weight each day, swifts circle overhead and devour any insect that's small enough to eat, including thousands of mosquitoes and other pests that would otherwise bite or sting us or consume our gardens and ornamentals.

Swifts are so fast and facile—veering and darting along paths that are hard to follow—that they have few predators, save the agile merlin and peregrine falcon, or the occasional sharp-shinned hawk.

These indefatigable birds seldom land, except to roost at night and when nesting. Moved by the mating urge, they circle in small groups, ramping up their speed and level of chatter. Consummation, which generally takes place in the nest site, lasts but a few seconds while the male raises his wings and makes contact with the female. On occasion, swifts will mate in mid-air, often following an aerial pas de deux during which the amorous pair raise their wings in a V-shape and glide down together in curving flight.

In New England, swifts make their nests from late April to May, using small twigs that they snap off with their feet while in flight. The swift then transfers each twig to its mouth and uses mucilaginous saliva to glue it into

*Chimney swift.*

a half-nest that adheres to the chimney wall. Both sexes build the nest. Although sharp claws and bristly tails help them to cling to vertical surfaces, swifts cannot perch on a branch or even stand on a flat surface. Nests can be constructed from near the top of a chimney to more than 20 feet down the flue. Occasionally, swifts will nest in cisterns and silos, along barn walls, or even in outhouses.

Each tiny nest soon holds four to five pure-white eggs, which hatch in 18 to 19 days. A month after hatching, the fledglings climb to the top of the chimney and take to the sky. Breeding pairs raise only one brood each year. In early August, swifts congregate in anticipation of the journey south.

Our favorite time to watch swifts is when their tireless flights teach young birds the secrets of survival and reinforce their ebullient nature. Swifts create one of the greatest spectacles to behold in the sky above our neighborhoods. At dusk they swirl above the roosting chimney to form a living avian funnel. Each bird circles until just the right moment, when it lifts up its wings, angles its tail, then checks its flight before alighting delicately down the flue.

Although a late-spring chill can occasionally wipe out the swift's essential insect food for a time, people pose a far greater threat. When a fire is built in a chimney with nests, the heat and smoke can wipe out an entire roost of hundreds or thousands of birds.

The lack of chimneys in many contemporary houses, as well as the construction materials used in newer chimneys, also present problems, as Cornell's Laura Erickson observes. "Populations of chimney swifts have declined throughout their range as metal-lined chimneys have replaced their brick counterparts. There's nothing to hang on to inside a metal-lined chimney. Even new brick chimneys have liners that chimney swifts can't hang on to."

If you have a masonry chimney, you can manage the flue to make it safe for swifts. Clean the chimney after the wood-burning season, keep the top open from late April to early September so swifts can gain access, and don't light fires when they're around. If you're really motivated, you can obtain plans for building a swift nesting tower at www.chimneyswifts.org.

And however you like to spend your late summer days, keep your eyes on the sky as dusk settles in. With a bit of luck, you may witness the swifts' crepuscular choreography as they spiral in ever-smaller circles across a ruddy sky.

# That's the Nature of Coyotes, Deer

MANY INDIGENOUS TALES PORTRAY the coyote as a trickster, and for good reason. Here is an animal so highly adaptable it can survive in environments ranging from deep woods to suburbia. Adding to the mystique of this wild member of the canid family, coyotes are mostly seen and heard in the wan light of dawn and dusk—moments that many people associate with danger and the unknown.

In recent years, the crepuscular wailing of coyotes has become as much a part of autumn in New England as falling leaves and wood smoke. But coyote voices are not music to everyone's ears. Deer hunters, in particular, often view coyotes as unwelcome competitors and associate their howling with a lost prize.

"Coyotes howl to communicate with each other, not to hunt," says Susan Morse, founder and director of Keeping Track in Huntington, Vermont. She has spent many years studying coyotes in the wild. "Calls are often between mothers and pups of the year. It's ludicrous to think that the howls in the night are some sort of pre-kill call to arms. Predators know better than that. Secrecy and stealth are key."

Depending on the season and availability, coyotes eat a wide variety of foods, including rabbits, insects, squirrels, turkeys, muskrats, songbirds, poultry, beavers, woodchucks, and deer. In wetter areas, coyotes will partake of frogs, turtles, snakes, lizards, and crayfish, with small rodents—including mice and meadow voles—always on the menu. Coyotes also consume a number of plant foods. I once watched a coyote devour a large patch of mushrooms

*Coyote howling.*

in a matter of minutes and have also noticed that, when wild apples ripen and are falling from the trees, coyote scat is replete with the remains of this abundant fruit.

Cunning and resilient, coyotes do what they must to survive. "Coyotes sometimes hunt alone, sometimes with a few together in family groups," says Morse. "In northern New England, coyotes have evolved social behaviors to help them hunt larger game."

A coyote's keen senses of sight, sound, and smell help it to locate prey. When a coyote finds a mouse or other small animal, it stalks and then pounces. Coyotes rush and chase down larger prey.

"Coyotes eat just about anything," says Charles W. Johnson, Vermont's retired state naturalist. "They're like a big version of the fox." In fact, when food is scarce, coyotes have been known to kill red foxes living within their home range in order to decrease the competition for food.

"Coyotes are opportunistic and omnivorous with a capital O, and their effect on deer can vary by place and season, and from year to year," says Morse. "They eat a lot of berries in summer: cherries, viburnums, huckleberries,

blueberries, and raspberries. The red dripping from a coyote's mouth isn't necessarily blood: just as often, it's berry juice."

After the snow falls, coyotes spend long periods of time resting to save scarce energy reserves. When they do hunt, they conserve energy and avoid breaking new trails in deep snow. Coyote tracks often follow snow trails that have been established by deer or hares, even matching deer tracks print-for-print and traveling in single file.

Hares and rabbits are important coyote foods in winter, a time when coyotes may eat three times more carrion—in the form of deer, moose, and domestic animals—than in summer. Most of the time, coyotes catch individual or lone animals that are smaller, slower, and weaker than other members of their group.

"In habitat with deep snow and during long, cold winters, when temperatures routinely dip to 20 to 30 degrees below zero, deer are of necessity confined to deer winter range areas, and this can invite coyote predation," Morse says. "In winter, and near the end of winter and early spring, the deer that aren't doing well aren't going to make it anyway. They'll likely starve and then be eaten by a coyote. And there's no question that coyotes also successfully kill other deer on the winter range."

Deer populations, like those of coyotes, are largely determined by available food and not just by the forces of predation. When there is an ample food supply, deer populations will remain healthy despite predation from coyotes.

Jonathan G. Way of Boston College's department of environmental studies has extensively researched coyote behavior in southern New England. He has observed that, "Coyotes hunt the most vulnerable animals, which tend to be fawns and older deer. But something that makes a prime deer susceptible, such as a wound from a gunshot or collision with a car, can make that animal vulnerable as well. However, killing a large mammal like a deer is not an easy undertaking. Rather, it is dangerous, and, likely, some coyotes die from these attempts."

According to Way, hunting coyotes can upset their population balance, and not in the way most hunters expect. "Coyotes live at low densities, probably in groups of three to four in well over 10 square miles in the North Country. Killing coyotes actually opens up a territory for others. We have evidence on Cape Cod that doing that can actually cause an increase in coyote numbers in a local area as an unguarded territory is claimed by more than one group." Because coyote populations are food-limited, killing coyotes simply invites new coyotes to move in and take over the food supply.

Says Morse: "People are a menace to deer insofar as our thoughtless development patterns and irresponsible logging practices can remove and/or degrade deer habitat considerably. In so doing, we render deer more susceptible to predation by coyotes and, just as often, our own domestic dogs. It behooves us, therefore, to conserve adequate quality habitat for deer so that the impact of predation is more natural and balanced."

# Endearing, Enterprising

## THE EASTERN CHIPMUNK

A CHIPMUNK'S IS THE ONLY LIFE I have ever saved using CPR (see "Prologue"). That chippy's seeming return from the dead remains one of my most astounding encounters with the natural world, and reinforces the animal's reputation as being full of spunk and grit. In one traditional Aniyunwiya (Cherokee) story, the animals wanted to retaliate against human beings for hunting them. They decided to inflict sickness and disease upon people. But a recalcitrant Chipmunk said he had nothing against the two-leggeds and refused to go along with the plan, so the other animals attacked him. In the midst of the fight, Bear raked his paw down Chipmunk's back and left claw marks there.

The two words that comprise the chipmunk's Latin name, *Tamias striatus*, mean "treasurer/storer" and "striped/furrowed." A black stripe runs down the center of a chipmunk's ruddy brown back, highlighted on each side by a white stripe bordered with black. A white stripe also runs above and below each eye, with a black line through the eye. A chipmunk's wispy tail is 3 to 4 inches long.

We often see a chippy near our house grooming its small, rounded ears by rubbing its front paws against them, revealing four toes and a tiny thumb. Although "our" chippy resides under a large stone stoop, natural chipmunk habitat includes forests, the edges of woodlands, brushy fields, stone walls, and hedgerows. Chipmunks frequently live under rocks, logs, and stumps or in fieldstone foundations.

Chipmunks use their acute sense of smell to find seeds, including acorns, hickory nuts, beechnuts, and hazelnuts. They also eat wild berries, grain,

domestic fruits, mushrooms, pumpkins, and other squash. But chipmunks aren't strict vegetarians. They'll consume worms, insects, frogs, eggs, and small animals like mice, songbirds, and snakes. Chipmunk predators include snakes, hawks, foxes, cats, and people, especially disgruntled gardeners. I once saw a red squirrel dangling a headless chipmunk between its crimson lips.

One dedicated mammalogist determined that a chipmunk's cheek pouches have a maximum capacity of 70 sunflower seeds, 31 corn kernels, or 12 acorns. The food is pushed into the cheeks through gaps between the lateral teeth. A chipmunk's goal is to cache enough food to carry it through the winter and into the spring, storing the food in underground burrows that are about 10 feet long and 3 feet deep. In addition to a main entrance, several other passages are dug as emergency escapes but are normally kept blocked.

Chipmunks are most active in spring and autumn. They lay low in the heat of summer and eat very little. When winter arrives, they block the den door and hibernate, curled up in a dry bed of leaves. Wintering chipmunks wake once in a while to raid their pantries. The den's living area is kept clean: droppings, nutshells, and other waste are stored in special tunnels. Dormant chippies occasionally come above ground in mild winter spells. I have seen one foraging near its den in the first week of February.

When maple sap starts to rise, male chipmunks wake up, find a female, and swish their tails in courtship. About a month later, four to five hairless young are born. Chiplets open their eyes after four weeks and become independent a month after that. Chipmunk adults sometimes breed again in midsummer, with the next generation ready to start breeding the following year. On average, chipmunks survive for two or three years.

Most of us know the familiar "chip" they make when we startle them and they flee to cover with tails bolt upright. Ever curious, they soon poke their heads up again to get a closer look at the imminent threat.

Chipmunks defend territories of roughly a quarter acre in size. They do this by making a repetitive, low-range, territorial "chuck, chuck" to mark their feeding grounds—a circle around the burrow with a radius of about 75 feet. Chippies often scuffle with their neighbors and chase them out of their territories.

By gathering and burying seeds, chipmunks aid in the spread of trees, shrubs, and other plants. When partaking of fungi, they disperse the spores of species that aid tree roots in the absorption of nutrients. Chipmunks also spread the reproductive spores of truffles.

Although chipmunks are endearing and entertaining, not everyone is enamored of them. Gardeners, for example, know that hungry chipmunks don't discriminate between wild and cultivated plants. To avoid conflicts in the garden, make sure all seeds (grass seed, bird-feeder seed, vegetable

seeds) are stored in chipmunk-proof containers, both protecting the seeds and preventing a large population of chipmunks from growing up around the free fare. Use quarter-inch hardware cloth around especially prized plants to keep the chipmunks out. It may also help to maintain a gap between the edge of the woods and any ornamental plantings so that the chipmunks don't have unbroken cover as access to flowerbeds and gardens. And finally, keep bird feeders away from buildings and collections of ornamental plants that are likely to suffer from proximity to chipmunks.

If all else fails in the face of your resident chipmunk's guile and determination, it may be time to consider an alternative approach. One Native American tradition involves planting a large extra measure of whatever you are growing—so that you will have enough left over after the chipmunks and other critters have had their fill.

# Woodcocks in Mudtime

WHEN MUD SEASON ARRIVES, I go out at sunset wearing khakis and a brown checked jacket. I wait in the brush of a hedgerow that trails down to a wet meadow. The sky turns salmon, then fades to gray as stars begin to flicker.

From the edge of the field comes a ventriloquist-like series of *peents* that are repeated just seconds apart. Now they sound near, now far, now near again. From up close, I have seen a male woodcock turn some 90 degrees in between each *peent*, projecting his voice in different directions to attract potential mates.

After about five minutes of calling, a chunky bird rises. Wings whistle as the bird spirals high into the dusk. The flight soon peaks and the bird descends on warbling wing beats, landing back in the same spot. The *peenting* resumes.

The bird in question is the woodcock, the great mud-season aerialist of New England. Woodcocks are famous for crepuscular displays and nocturnal foraging. Their habit of haunting wet places during the mysterious hours of dusk has inspired colorful names: night peck, night partridge, timberdoodle, bogsucker, Labrador twister, and, my favorite, hookum pake.

I once lay down a few feet from where a woodcock was about to land. The bird fluttered down but saw me. Caught between the drive to flee and a desire to continue the courtship, he emitted a cooing *woodle* each time his head bobbed, sandpiper-like. The timberdoodle tried to resume his mating ritual but couldn't ignore my intrusion.

Woodcocks have a thick neck and a long, straight bill set in a smallish head dominated by enormous eyes. They can grow to 11 inches in length, including their beak. Their feathers sport a leaf-like camouflage of mottled browns and flecks of black above, with pale orange-brown below.

*American woodcock.*

These magnificent birds move on stout legs as they search for food in loam, mud, and leaf litter. Like others in the sandpiper family, the woodcock employs strong jaw muscles and a long, sensitive bill to probe the soil. The prehensile tip of the brownish bill can be opened to grasp prey while the rest of the bill remains closed. This is accomplished by muscles at the front of the skull that control a bone that runs the length of the upper bill. When this long bone is pushed forward, the bill's flexible tip bends up and open while the shorter, lower bill remains fixed.

Earthworms comprise 50 to 90 percent of a woodcock's food, with most of the rest being larvae, beetles, grasshoppers, flies, crustaceans, spiders, centipedes, and millipedes. Up to a tenth of their diet is vegetable material, such as berries and seeds from blackberries, ragweed, violets, sedges, knotweed, and grasses.

Woodcocks overwinter in southeastern and south-central states, but they breed throughout much of eastern North America, north to Newfoundland and west to southern Manitoba. They are found in grassy fields, abandoned farmland, logged and burned areas, low-lying woods, wet meadows, and shrubby forest edges. Search for them in groves of aspen, birch, and red maple less than 25 feet tall, preferably with evergreens in the understory. Woodcocks also frequent alder and willow swales along the margins of streams and ponds.

Look for the woodcock's aerial mating display on flat to gently sloping sites, often at the edges of old fields, pastures, and farmland. I never approach too close to any particular woodcock more than once in a mating season. After a male is frightened away, he doesn't resume courtship until the next evening. Repeated disturbance causes males to abandon a site for the season.

It is especially hard to sneak up on a woodcock because their eyes are set back and high on the head so that they can see while feeding with the bill stuck in the ground. Wide fields of vision overlap at front and rear to create a rare attribute: simultaneous binocular vision both forward and backward.

This also helps the parent keep watch while incubating eggs in the nest—an unlined, leafy depression on the ground. Nests are usually located in shrubby bottomland forest or open, young to middle-aged deciduous forest near water. Sometimes nests are found at the brushy edge of an open field or on a wetland hummock. The three or four buff to grayish-white eggs are speckled with pale, reddish-brown spots. Woodcock chicks are precocial—they leave the nest, walk and eat on their own soon after hatching. Tiny, down-covered woodcocklings are all head and eyes.

If the young are threatened, their mother darts erratically, creating a diversion while the chicks escape into the underbrush. Then she disappears, camouflaged with the background. A mother is said to be able to carry a chick to safety by holding it tightly between her feet or thighs and flying away.

It may be the woodcock's bizarre appearance that many find so intriguing, but for me it's the suspense of an encounter with a wild creature at dusk, the bewitching hour, at a time of year that can otherwise be bleak and forlorn.

PLANTS

# *Blooming Heat*

SKUNK CABBAGE TURNED

ON BY POLLINATION

EVERY YEAR, IN MID-MARCH, my family leaves Vermont and heads to Massachusetts' Pioneer Valley to get a jump on experiencing spring. Red-winged blackbirds are calling, chipmunks are foraging, and flocks of robins abound. Bending down to smell the first subtle scents of crocuses and daffodils, we give thanks that winter is over. Sometimes, we also take a whiff of skunk cabbage flowers, just for the olfactory shock value.

Anyone who has ever stooped down to sniff a blooming skunk cabbage would agree that it measures up to the Latin name, *Symplocarpus foetidus*. The flower and crushed leaves emanate a "fetid" skunk-like odor. Not surprisingly, some of the insects drawn to skunk cabbage blooms are also attracted to carrion. The genus *Symplocarpus* means "single fruit," for each flower produces a ball of small, one-seeded fruits.

Skunk cabbage grows throughout the Northeast and Midwest, ranging from North Carolina well up into the northernmost reaches of Quebec. The flower emerges through the snow and ice of March in the understory of wooded swamps, along riverbanks, lakeshores, and in other habitats with rich wet soils. First growth is an exotic, crimson-hued, 3- to 6-inch tall cowl—called a *spathe*—that surrounds and protects a spherical cluster of flowers. Each flower measures ¾-inch across and consists of 50 to 100 tightly packed florets.

Seeing a skunk cabbage poke through the snow, it's easy to assume that its

dark color has absorbed the sun's heat and melted a ring around itself, much like bark does around a tree. But the plant's behavior is as exotic as its appearance. During the two-week period when the male flowers are pollinating and female flowers are receptive to being pollinated, the sex organs of the flower generate their own serious heat.

In 1974 biologist Roger Knutson discovered that skunk cabbage flowers can maintain a temperature that's significantly higher than the air surrounding them. Another field study conducted in Ontario during the month of March found that when the outside temperature is just 37 degrees, the air inside the spathe is maintained at a balmy 61 degrees. When the air temperature drops below 37 degrees, the flowers can't produce enough heat to keep up, but they don't freeze until exposed to 14 degrees or below.

Plants respire just like animals do, and skunk cabbage produces energy from the starch stored in its roots. During their pollination phase, skunk cabbage flowers consume as much oxygen, by mass, as a shrew or hummingbird. As air temperature falls, the skunk cabbage responds by increasing its metabolism and heat production.

This self-generated warmth promotes early pollination, protects flowers from freeze and frost, mobilizes the flower's fetid scent, and provides a haven for early-season insects. To an insect's sensitive olfaction, each putrid plume is an irresistible perfume beckoning it to enter. Pollen-gathering honeybees, in particular, are attracted to the most odoriferous skunk cabbage flowers. Some conjecture that the flowers may also mimic the heat generated by a rotting corpse as an additional lure for carrion-eaters.

Our native skunk cabbage, of the family *Araceae*, is among just a handful of heat-generating or *thermogenic* species of plants in existence. For example, the cut-leaf philodendron (*Philodendron selloum*) of the southern Brazilian rainforest burns fat to maintain a temperature of 114 degrees during its two-day flowering period. Another heat-producing relative is the European arum lily (*Arum maculatum*). In all of these plants, heat production is timed to coincide with blooming and pollination.

So when you see a skunk cabbage melting through the snow, you can be sure it's pollinating. Bend down and gently feel the heat of the flower. There, at ground level where the wind is fairly calm, a faint circulation pattern flows as the lighter, warmer air rises out the top of the spathe and the colder, heavier air enters below.

You may also see some of the many species that take advantage of this plant's micro-environment. In addition to pollen-gathering honeybees and carrion-eating insects such as flies, a number of other invertebrates are drawn to skunk cabbage flowers. Springtails, beetles, sow bugs, true bugs, and the larvae of butterflies and moths have been discovered in these outposts of nourishment. And where insects visit, spiders are sure to follow. Ironically, insects lured in by the smell of death, may lose their lives in the pursuit.

# Beyond the Pussy Willow

## EARLY SPRING WILDFLOWERS

SOON AFTER MOVING to Vermont in 1981, I began to hear a common lament, delivered with a slow shake of the head and a sigh of Yankee resignation. "There's no springtime here. We go from winter right into summer, not like down south where spring lasts for months."

While our vernal season does move quickly, spring stretches longer here than most people realize. Beyond the first steam that rises from sugaring shacks, the return of red-winged blackbirds, and the calls of wood frogs, there are subtle harbingers awaiting those who seek out our earliest blooms.

Pussy willows, those fuzzy forerunners of full flowers, are a welcome sight in the wetlands of April. A Native American story tells of a rabbit that jumped up into a willow shrub from atop the winter's deepest snows. He was so exhausted from a day of leaping that he nestled in the crotch of a high branch and slept away the rest of the winter. The snows melted. When this Rabbit Van Winkle awoke and looked down from what was then a great height, he became dizzy and fell. As he plummeted, tiny bits of fuzz from his tail caught and tore off on the tips of each branch. Ever since that day, pussy willow flower buds have borne spring coats of fur.

Late snows and freezing rains often cover the outside of each willow bud's jacket, which protects the growing flower parts within. When these flowers mature, they produce a bounty of mustard-colored pollen that is an important food for honeybees, moths, and other insects that buzz from bloom to bloom. These early spring visitors team up with the wind to help spread pollen at a time when there are no leaves to inhibit the breeze that blows through the branches.

You'll need a pair of binoculars to view another jewel of the plant world: wildflowers on high that sometimes emerge before the pussy willow. Focus up in the branches of silver maple to see its tiny flowers. In Vermont, I have recorded the appearance of the red female blooms and reddish-yellow male flowers on the first day of April. A popular shade tree, silver maple grows naturally along the edges of wetlands and rivers. In mid to late April, when the flowers have gone by, their remnants fall as nondescript squiggly things that pile up on cars and sidewalks. Later in the summer, maple seed *samaras* or *keys* detach and spiral down like small whirligigs.

*Maple flowers.*

As early as March 31, American hazelnuts bloom beneath the filtered shade of hedgerows and in moist forests. The dangling male catkins are easy to find, but you'll need to look backward through your binoculars—using them as a hand lens—to explore the diminutive female blossoms of this delicate shrub, whose petals shoot from the bud like a burst of floral fireworks. It takes three of these crimson beauties, stretched petal to petal, to reach across the face of a dime. These flowers will eventually form hazelnuts, or filberts.

Focus again in the treetops to see two of our earliest bloomers. The dangling, fuzzy flowers of popple (also called poplar or aspen) precede the familiar quaking, pea-green leaves. I have seen several chunky ruffed grouse perched incongruously in the leafless crowns of aspen while feasting on the delicate blooms. Each aspen tree, like holly and willow, bears either male or female flowers. Aspens can also propagate by root sprouts, and sometimes a grove spreads out from one parent tree to form a giant clone. Watch for the cottony tufts that drift down when the mature seeds begin to disperse.

A fellow naturalist I know argues that all of these florid events take a back seat, in both timing and splendor, to the display of our beloved and embattled American elm, whose purplish flowers are among the most precocious. Whichever flower is your favorite, spring begins early and lasts long for anyone who takes the time to develop an eye for the intricate beauty of these first flowers of the season, our vernal garden in the sky.

# Explosive Seeds and Spores

Q: Why did the witch hazel cross the street?
A: To grow on the other side.

OF COURSE shrubs can't really cross the street, but their seeds can. The seeds of witch hazel are shot out of capsules with such force that they travel up to 40 feet. We tend to think of seed dispersal as a passive enterprise, with a germ of the next generation carried aloft on tiny parasols, hitchhiking within burrs that are stuck to fur or feather, or dropping onto the surface of water to drift away and sprout in distant soil. But witch hazel is one of many kinds of plants and fungi that can actively expel their seeds or spores a considerable distance by employing various forms of compression chambers, coiled green springs, and catapults.

Some years ago, I was leading teachers on a summer field trip through the Philbrick-Cricenti bog in New London, New Hampshire. After marveling at the carnivorous pitcher plants, sundews, and bladderworts, we sat down along the trail to eat our own lunch near a large patch of sphagnum moss. When the sunlight beamed through a hole in the tree crowns and shone on the moss's tiny red spore cases, they began to blow their little caps off. Each capsule emitted an audible "pop" as it spewed a minute puff of spores into the bright air. Sphagnum spore cases shrink as they mature, increasing the pressure inside to as high as 5 atmospheres until they flip their tops and spill the spores. This is equivalent to the pressure that an ocean diver experiences at a depth of 165 feet.

Certain kinds of mushrooms also use pressure to shoot their spores out, in this case from between their gills. This helps to mobilize the spores and move them up out of the still air near the ground and into the wind. Cup fungi grow spores in structures that absorb moisture as they mature, increasing the pressure inside. Eventually, and often en masse, these structures erupt and release a smoky cloud of spores that waft on the breeze.

Jewelweed, or "touch-me-not," is perhaps the most well-known seed-thrower. The orange or yellow, cornet-shaped flowers form thin, inch-long seedpods. Gently pinch the end of one of the ripe, swollen pods, and five tensile plant springs instantly separate and unfurl to fling the seeds a good distance. In an essay titled, "The Dispersion of Seeds," Henry David Thoreau aptly described this phenomenon: "Touch-me-not seed vessels, as all know, go off like pistols at the slightest touch, and so suddenly and energetically that they always startle you, though you are expecting it."

The round-leaved yellow violet squeezes its seeds in a way that is similar to how we shoot watermelon seeds by pinching them between the tips of our fingers until they fly. As the violet's three-parted seed capsule ripens, then dries, it gradually compresses the seeds until they are spit out, one at a time, with some traveling nearly 10 feet.

Certain members of the pea family also sling their seeds. As the pods of wild vetch mature and dry, the inner lining shrinks more than the outer layer, which generates a tension between the two layers. Eventually, this tension causes the pod to split lengthwise down the sides, and each half of the pod snaps into a coiled shape, flipping the seeds outward. Soak the halves of the open pod in water, and they will resume their original shape.

Another legume, called birds-foot trefoil, forms beautiful, pea-like yellow flowers in midsummer. Flowers mature into narrow, inch-long, brownish-black seedpods that radiate out from the stem in a pattern that resembles the toes on a bird's

Witch Hazel

Pinesap                    Indian pipe

At the tip of each stem, Indian pipe grows a waxy, inch-long flower bearing four to five small petals. Young flowers face earthward on the end of down-turned stalks. This familiar silhouette reminded colonists of the ceremonial pipes or *calumets* of New England's indigenous cultures. Indeed the Abenakis of Northern New England and Quebec noticed this similarity long ago and named the plant *odamôganiz*, or "a little pipe."

Flowers appear on this perennial from June through September and are a source of nectar for bumblebees. Once the young flowers become pollinated and begin to form seeds, they turn up to face the sun. This habit gave rise to the Latin name of *Monotropa* ("once-turned") *uniflora* ("one-flowered.")

Although fairy smoke, as it is sometimes also called, lacks chlorophyll and can't create food energy from sunlight, it is a true flowering plant. The silken white flowers are so bright that they appear almost radiant in the shadowy woodlands where they grow.

While they don't glow in the dark, as some people believe, Indian pipe *can* grow in the dark—because it absorbs its needed energy from the fungi in a rich forest floor. The *Russula* and *Lactarius* mushrooms that Indian pipes parasitize are called *mycorrhizal* fungi; they have a mutually beneficial relationship with many tree species, including birches, beeches, and some conifers. Fungal threads penetrate tree roots, expanding the roots' abilities to absorb nutrients from the soil. In turn, the tree roots pass water and carbohydrates to the fungi.

This complicated relationship has been explored by botanists who treated the sugars in trees with radioactive isotopes. The scientists then traced the passage of these sugars from the tree roots, though the mycorrhizal fungi, and into the parasitic Indian pipes. In this case, the fungi inadvertently act as surrogate nutrient thieves for the pilfering pipes.

Pinesap, a close relative of Indian pipe, is also a nutrient bandit. The roots of pinesap parasitize *Tricholoma*, another genus of mycorrhizal fungi. Pinesap inhabits the acid soils of our pine and oak forests; its Latin name is *Monotropa hypopithys* ("under pines"). It bears clusters of three to ten, cream- to lavender-colored flowers on fuzzy stems that are pale pink or sometimes even yellowish. The delicate, half-inch blossoms are bell-shaped. In his fascinating book, *A Naturalist Buys an Old Farm*, Edwin Way Teale describes an encounter with pinesap as like coming "upon clumps of Indian pipes that, instead of being waxy ghostly white, are a beautiful shade of pink, sometimes with the color even deepening into red." If you should come upon Indian pipe or pinesap on your next woodland foray, you may be tempted to pick a few and bring them home for a closer look. But resist the urge, because neither is a keeper. Soon after being picked, they wither and turn black. Nature's mysterious ghost plants are best appreciated when left undisturbed to thrive in their own native haunts.

# Green Defenses

## HOW PLANTS FIGHT BACK

THE NEXT TIME you wander into a patch of stinging nettles, or contract a bad case of urushiol-induced contact dermatitis (poison ivy), try to see things from the plant's point of view. Our green neighbors get picked, eaten, infected, or uprooted by any number of organisms, including people, insects and other herbivores, fungi, bacteria, and viruses. What's a plant to do?

Defend itself.

Plants use spines, bristles, toxins, and irritants as green armor. The noxious oil of poison sumac leaves and berries causes skin to itch and blister. Coatings of silica, wax, and resins make leaves and stems distasteful and indigestible. Blackberry thorns send a painful message: "Eat the berries and spread the seeds, but leave the plants alone!"

Insects are especially adept at penetrating botanical foils. For millions of years, the six-leggeds have engaged in a duel of genetic thrusts and parries with plants—an epic battle between Earth's most numerous species and those with the world's greatest living mass. One theory purports that the arms race between plants and herbivores is a major force behind the development of their phenomenal diversity.

Many plants possess potent alkaloids that inhibit insect digestion and metabolism, interrupt nerve impulses, weaken cells, and even cause cell walls to leak. We have adopted many of these alkaloids for medicine or as mind-altering drugs, including nicotine, caffeine, strychnine, quinine, morphine, and mescaline. Mandrake root contains an alkaloid called scopolamine that poisons some plant eaters but quells motion sickness in humans.

Other familiar insecticides from plants—both helpful and harmful to humans—include menthol, camphor, latex, citronella, cannabis, cocaine, opium, benzoin, and gum resins. Steroids and vitamin D were originally derived from insect-fighting plant compounds. Pyrethrin, a natural insecticide found in chrysanthemums, is concentrated and sold for pest control.

Chemical precursors to salicylic acid, or aspirin, are found in the sap of tobacco and in other familiar plants, such as willow, teaberry, and both black and yellow birch. Plants concentrate salicylic acid when they are attacked, using it as we do—as an anti-inflammatory to fight infections caused by viruses and other microbes. The powerful cancer-fighting compound Taxol is found in the bark of the pacific yew, in common hazelnut, and in fungi associated with hazelnut.

Some defensive plant compounds are extremely toxic to humans. Pokeweed roots, leaf stalks, and berries, with their attractive purple hues, contain lectin—a protein that causes red blood cells to clot. Lectin is also found in the deadly ricin of castor beans. As few as a dozen berries from a nightshade can be fatal to a child. Foxglove, lily of the valley, oleander, and baneberry produce cardiac glycosides that can cause heart failure. Because children think that colorful leaves and berries look good to eat, nearly 60 percent of all individuals poisoned by glycosides are under seven years old.

*Blackberry.*

Even with these impressive fortifications, plants must continuously adapt. Each time a plant develops a new line of defense, its foes probe for a way around it. When the halo blight bacterium invades a bean plant, for example, a protein alerts the victim and triggers the bean's immune response. The bacterium then throws a genetic switch that stops production of that protein, and so invades undetected.

But plants also have a few tricks up their proverbial sleeves. When the fungus-like *Phytophthora sojae* attacks, parsley activates a toxic chemical defense. Tomato plants under siege produce greater amounts of a chemical that inhibits the digestion of proteins in insect larvae, causing the ubiquitous leaf-munchers to become undernourished. Certain plants even grow thorns in response to grazing.

Plant defenses are ingenious, intricate, and tailor-made to defeat those who would harm them. Mouth fluids from caterpillars that eat corn, tobacco, and cotton can cause the entire plant to emit a chemical scent that attracts insect parasites which, in turn, attack the offending caterpillars. Each different kind of larva causes the victimized plant to emanate the specific scent needed to lure that pest's parasites.

Some plant roots can discern whether invading fungi are hurtful or helpful. Detrimental fungi are attacked as soon as they invade root tissues. But when the root senses a mycorrhizal fungus—the beneficial kind that expands the root's ability to absorb nutrients from the soil—the plant suppresses its counterattack and allows the fungal threads to penetrate.

Like these symbiotic fungi, people often help to nourish plants that we find useful. Cultivation under optimal growing conditions and in healthy soil creates vigorous plants that can protect themselves while attracting insects that work to our advantage.

With or without our help, plants have proven resilient over time. Now, however, they must adapt to challenges posed by rapid climate change. Fossil records of trees show that, when the climate warms, the rate at which insects consume deciduous leaves increases, as does the number of different kinds of insects doing the damage. Time will tell how global warming will tip the delicate balance in the struggle between plants and their ravenous foes.

WINTER

# A Burst of Boreal Birds

IN YEARS WHEN WINTER FOOD IS SCARCE in the boreal forests of Canada, flocks of birds migrate south and *irrupt* or "burst" upon local fields, forests, and feeders. The winter of 2007–2008 brought flocks of purple finches, pine siskins, pine grosbeaks, and evening grosbeaks to New England. Red-breasted nuthatches were on the move, as were predatory northern shrikes. Bird watchers will long recall the now legendary irruption of snowy owls during the winter of 2013–2014.

The boreal forests are vast woodlands, dominated by northern conifers, that grow south of the tundra. Many birds that normally overwinter there will migrate south when food is short, flying hundreds or even thousands of miles. Flocks of finches scatter widely, while some predators, such as the northern shrike, often return to the same winter location. So-called *superflight* occurs when large numbers from many species irrupt during the same winter over a widespread geographical range.

Avian irruptions don't foretell a hard winter, nor are they a response to extreme cold. Northern birds are hardy: redpolls can endure temperatures of −60 degrees Fahrenheit. But that's only if they have enough food to keep their metabolisms stoked. Whenever food supplies are low, either due to a poor seed crop or an unusually successful breeding season (leading to food scarcity), an irruption is likely to take place.

Because each species prefers certain foods, irruptions depend on which northern foods are in short supply. Among the different finches, crossbills eat the seeds of conifers while redpolls prefer birch and alder catkins. So these two finches won't necessarily irrupt during the same winter. For similar reasons, the movements of finches often don't overlap with those of black-capped chickadees, boreal chickadees, red-breasted nuthatches, or Bohemian waxwings.

And don't get the idea that boreal birds are food-flighty—departing at the first sign of shortage. Animals prepare well for the cold, preserve their energy stores, and only undertake a long winter journey when normal feeding behavior won't suffice. Many birds mitigate the dangers of food scarcity by stashing food for later use. Gray jays or "whiskey jacks" use saliva to glue their food to tree trunks and branches above the normal snowline. Chickadees store considerable quantities of seeds, insects, spiders, and other foods by jamming them into bark crevices and other nooks. Research has shown that chickadees may cache up to 100,000 morsels of food each year, and that, using visual cues, they are able to recall where they put their food for up to several weeks.

On one late December day in 1981, during a heavy snowstorm, I encountered a flock of pine grosbeaks feeding on dried crabapples along Pleasant Street in Woodstock, Vermont, evoking the image of live holiday ornaments adorning the trees. Like many boreal birds, pine grosbeaks are inordinately tame: I approached within a few feet of the sleek, rose-feathered males and elegant, gray, yellow-rumped females. Pine grosbeaks don't travel very far south in winter, often settling in northern states where there are enough dried berries, ash buds, and seeds. The demeanor of these docile birds is in stark contrast to that of evening grosbeaks, whose bright colors complement their raucous nature. And while pine grosbeaks rarely ever alight at bird feeders, evening grosbeaks will invade en masse and drive other birds away.

Irrupting birds can't be distinguished from year-round residents of the same species because they look alike. Winter flocks of black-capped chickadees, blue jays, and American goldfinches may be a mélange of local birds mingled with those that migrated from farther north.

The unmistakable snowy owl only shows up in New England when the northern population of lemmings plummets. The periodic paucity of red-backed voles every three to five years can cause irruptions of great gray owls, boreal owls, and northern hawk owls. Similarly, rough-legged hawks will move farther south in greater numbers than usual when their rodent prey are scarce, as will northern shrikes when mouse numbers decline.

While taking a walk in early December 1995, I discovered a deer mouse impaled on the lance-like spike of a hawthorn. After catching their prey,

*Northern shrike eyes its prey.*

shrikes sever the spinal column with a fatal bite and store the carcass on a thorn, in the crotch of a tree, or even on barbed wire. I soon noticed that a new victim replaced the previous one every few days. The shrike often flew in and perched near its prey, but refused to eat while I was watching. The next shrike irruption occurred during the winter of 1999–2000.

Observing winter birds and their behavior is more than an interesting pastime. Citizen reports of bird sightings—logged online using such sites as ebird.org—enable ornithologists to keep track of avian wanderings over vast geographical ranges. Other records of winter birds come from participants in the Cornell Laboratory of Ornithology's Project FeederWatch and the National Audubon Society's Christmas Bird Count.

Tracking local irruptions is a wonderful way to enjoy winter birds. On December 11, 1855, Henry David Thoreau wrote: "When some rare northern bird like the pine grosbeak is seen thus far south in the winter, he does not suggest poverty, but dazzles us with his beauty . . . these rich but delicately tinted and hardy northern immigrants of the air."

# Cold Comfort for Trees

I WAS WORKING OUTSIDE during one of winter's warm spells, the kind of weather folks in the North Country call a "February thaw." The sun shone, and the temperature was in the low 40s. From the edge of the woods, a hopeful chickadee sang out, "phEE-bee, phEE-bee, phEE-bee." Winter was taking a breather.

After sunset, a weather front roared in with a bite. The temperature dropped quickly. I was hurrying to complete my work before dark, and the birds were drifting off to find shelter for the night, when a resonant *crack* rang out from the forest.

Somewhere on the steep riverbank a tree's bark had split, forming a vertical frost-crack along a length of the trunk. During mild, sunny winter weather, sunshine can warm the bark on the south and southwest sides of a tree up to 60 degrees Fahrenheit. If the temperature then drops too quickly, water in the wood and inner bark freezes and expands, causing the bark to split, often with a loud report, frequently causing damage beyond the bark to the cambium layer.

Rooted in place and unprotected from the vicissitudes of nature's harshest season, it's a wonder that trees can survive winter. Bark alone is no shield against sub-zero temperatures. An overwintering tree's situation is not unlike that of a cold-blooded animal or an insect, which also generate no heat of their own. Consider spring peepers: as cold weather descends, water exits their cells; the fluid that remains is largely glucose, which acts as a natural antifreeze.

As autumn begins and daylight hours are fewer, the membranes that surround the cells in tree tissues also start allowing water to pass through more freely. The water migrates out of cells and into the spaces between cell walls. Gradually, this water exerts pressure against the outside of the cell walls, but the pressure is offset as cells shrink and occupy less space.

As water exits, the cellular fluid that remains becomes concentrated with natural sugars, proteins, and organic acids. This lowers its freezing point. Eventually, as the weather becomes colder, ice crystals form in the water between cells; the expanding ice pushes on the cell membranes, but doesn't puncture them. So the tissues survive.

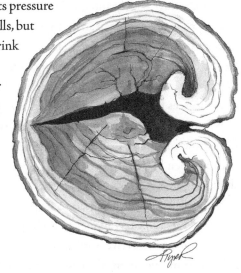

*Severe frost crack.*

Different types of trees thrive (or survive) at various northern latitudes depending in part on extreme winter temperatures. Sugar maple and black cherry generally can survive in temperatures to about −45 degrees, while yellow birch and white ash can handle nearly 50-below. Other species, such as eastern hemlock, white spruce, eastern cottonwood, and northern white cedar (arbor vitae), have been shown in experiments to possess a remarkable cold tolerance—far beyond temperatures they experience in nature. At the extreme were paper birch, balsam poplar, quaking aspen, balsam fir, and basswood, which was shown to survive temperatures of −112 degrees or below.

The cold tolerance of species with broad geographical ranges, such as red maple and American sycamore, depends on the climate where they grow. White pine in Tennessee dies when exposed to temperatures below −38 degrees, but tests have shown that some white pines growing in Minnesota could endure −128 degrees. At these extremes, even the minute amount of water remaining in a tree's cells can experience a deadly freeze. Alternatively, so much water can migrate outside the cells that they die of dehydration, or the organic substances that remain inside become concentrated to the point of toxicity.

During most winters, trees experience the greatest threat when the temperature swings widely and quickly. If autumn temperatures drop gradually, a tree's cell membranes can adapt to the changes. If an early, sudden cold snap appears before sufficient water has exited the cells, then the fluid within can freeze, expand, and burst those membranes, killing buds, twigs, or needles. On any given winter day, trees can cope with a temperature drop of as much as 20 degrees below the freezing point in an hour's time.

Winterkilled needles on pine, hemlock, spruce, and arbor vitae turn reddish-brown. Damage on deciduous trees may not show up until the growing season, when buds turn brown and leaves don't form, or when twigs die in the springtime.

There isn't much we can do to help wild trees survive the winter. There are, however, a few techniques to assist prized specimen trees to enter dormancy and safely survive until springtime, such as watering evergreens well in late autumn, wrapping the trunks of smooth-barked trees with burlap, and refraining from fertilizing trees after late summer, which could encourage a late growth spurt.

With the onset of March in New England, daytime temperatures rise above freezing. Sugar maples and other trees break their dormancy, and their roots again take up water from the soil. During the day, when sap begins to flow, some of it drizzles out of taps and into buckets or tubing. Farmers will collect the sap and boil it down to the elixir of the North Country. The delectable maple syrup that eventually tickles our taste buds may seem all the more sweet when we consider that the sugars we enjoy have helped the trees to survive the past winter's arctic blasts.

# Snug as a Snow Bug

ONE FROSTY WINTER'S DAY, while tracking a mink along the edge of a stream, I discovered some tiny winter stoneflies creeping on top of the snow. Unaccountably, the stream-dwelling larvae of these insects metamorphose into adults and emerge in the depths of winter. Feeding on algae, they move along the rocks, snow, and tree bark. After mating, females lay eggs in the stream. While we bundle up to ward off Jack Frost, these stark-naked little creatures remain unperturbed by winter's chill.

As a descendent of Mediterranean stock, I think monarch butterflies have got it right, making their epic journeys to a region where the climate is warm and dry. Populations from eastern and midwestern North America fly southwest each fall to central Mexico, where they roost on trees in the Sierra Madre mountains. Milkweed bugs and potato leafhoppers also migrate to balmier climes.

Those insects that remain in the North Country employ a variety of strategies for coping with winter. Like the winter stonefly, winter crane flies and the snow scorpionfly also crawl about when the thermometer rises above freezing. Their bodies can absorb the sun's heat, warming them to a tad above the ambient temperature.

But many insects assume the same body temperature as their surroundings and survive by entering a period of winter sleep called *diapause* ("stop between"), which is like hibernation but more complete. During diapause, their metabolism drops to one-tenth of normal and they live off fat stored during the growing season.

Some insects overwinter under leaf litter and in other sheltered spaces beneath the snow, resting in the cozy *subnivean* space (Latin for "under snow"),

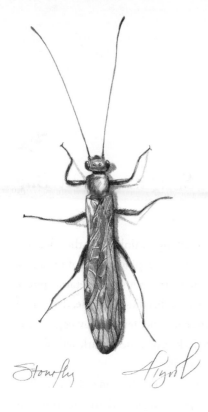

Stonefly *Pyrol*

where they find a measure of protection from extreme weather. Others spend the winter above the snow—in leaves, stems, and galls—exposed to the brunt of arctic blasts. The goldenrod gall fly can survive temperatures below −58 degrees Fahrenheit.

How do they endure such extremes? Many overwintering insects—including some butterflies, moths, bees, wasps, ants, beetles, flies, and midges—increase their cold tolerance as the temperature drops. Water migrates out of their cells and into the spaces between cells. When the water surrounding the cells freezes, it is not as likely to burst cell membranes and damage tissues. At the same time, concentrated sugars and alcohols—including glycerol, mannitol, sorbitol, and ethylene glycol—form within the cells, lowering their freezing point and keeping cellular fluids from icing up. This biological antifreeze enables the overwintering larvae of the arctic willow gall insect—whose winter weight is 20 percent glycerol—to survive polar air down to −90 degrees.

Certain invertebrates can elude freezing by lowering the volume of water both within *and* between their cells. Many overwinter in dry sites and expel the contents of their guts, so that no solid particles remain on which ice can crystallize. Some have waterproof pupal cases and exoskeletons. Using these adaptations, ticks, mites, spiders, and many insects won't freeze as long as the temperature stays above −4 degrees.

Each species of insect survives winter in a particular stage of its life cycle. Some enter diapause as adults, including mourning cloak butterflies, squash bugs, and ladybird beetles or "ladybugs," which cluster under leaves at the base of a tree or rock. This is also true of bumblebee, yellow jacket, and bald-faced hornet queens, which are the only individuals among these insects that live past autumn. Cricket and grasshopper eggs rest quietly in the soil. Walking sticks, eastern tent caterpillars, and most aphids also overwinter as eggs. For tiger swallowtails, owlet moths, and sphinx moths, it's the pupal stage that makes it through the cold season. Cicadas, dragonflies, and damselflies pass the winter as nymphs.

Fritillary butterflies and Isabella tiger moths winter as larvae. You might know the latter as the "woolly bears" that crawl about each autumn in search of a sheltered site to hibernate, sporting felt-like bands of black on each end and reddish-brown in the middle. These endearing caterpillars curl up for the winter but don't spin a cocoon and pupate until springtime.

When trying to maintain warmth and activity during the winter, there is strength in numbers. Ants, honeybees, and termites overwinter in nests. Honeybees, which evolved in the tropics, must store enough honey to provide the heat and energy needed to see the hive through to springtime. By clustering, a bee colony can maintain a temperature of 48 degrees Fahrenheit at the edge of the mass, and 86 to 95 degrees in the center. Termites and ants cope by moving deeper into the soil as the frost penetrates.

Meanwhile, winter stoneflies and others remain active in the frigid air. These fascinating insects possess a low *thermostupor point*—the temperature at which an animal becomes immobile. I can relate. After enduring more than three decades of Vermont winters, I've finally adapted: my own thermostupor point has fallen by a few degrees. Unfortunately, my general level of stupor has risen noticeably.

# A Muskrat Winter

WHENEVER I SEE THE EXPANSE of an icy marsh or a frozen bay in the bend of a river, dotted with the shelters of intrepid anglers, I shiver involuntarily. The wisps of smoke that drift up from the flues of the ice-fishing shacks bear testimony to the hardiness of those who enjoy this traditional North Country pastime.

But these anglers have company. Nearby, in the same quiet backwaters, muskrats have their own winter retreats—dome-shaped mounds of marsh plants fashioned above holes in the ice. Inside these shelters, the familiar dark-brown rodents, sometimes called "marsh rabbits," feed and rest during weather that would test the endurance and cold tolerance of even the most stalwart winter enthusiasts.

Each winter, when marshes freeze over, muskrats venture under the ice, swimming through well-traveled channels. While humans use gas-powered augers to drill holes in the ice, muskrats use their teeth. They gnaw four- to five-inch diameter holes and push marsh plants and mud up through the ice to form their mound shacks. Then they chew out the interior to create a place to eat, rest, and catch a breath of air after swimming under the ice. When a mound needs repairs, the holes are patched with everything from water lily roots to frozen catfish pulled from the mud.

Just as human anglers have regular homes, muskrats also have their own year-round dwellings. These typically rest on the bottom of the marsh, stick up above the water's surface, and often have several underwater doorways. Lodges are constructed of mud and plants, such as cattails. Muskrats build their lodges by piling up the plants, then chewing out an opening and carefully layering much of the removed material onto the top of the mound. Lodges can range from 3 to 5 feet wide, and up to 4 feet high. A family of roughly three to five muskrats lives in each lodge, with family members often hollowing out their own sleeping chambers. During the winter months, the temperature inside can be more than 30 degrees Fahrenheit above that of the outside world. Muskrats also may dig shelters into the banks of marshes, lakes, and the quiet backwaters of rivers.

Muskrats spend a lot of time in their winter homes and shacks—eating food from their autumn caches along with other marsh plants foraged under the ice. Because their heart rate decreases under water and oxygen is drawn from stores in muscle tissue, they can dive for more than 15 minutes to gather plants. Thick, waterproof fur keeps them dry and warm. The toes on their hind feet are partially webbed and fringed with stiff hairs, so they work like paddles. The muskrat's long tail undulates to provide additional propulsion when the animal swims; it also can be angled to act as a rudder.

Diving muskrats can gather food without swallowing water because their lips are able to close behind the two pairs of nearly inch-long upper and lower incisors, sealing out the cold water. Nimble front paws manipulate the roots of cattails, water lilies, arrowheads, pondweeds, and other marsh plants. They aren't strict vegetarians, and will also eat fish, clams, crayfish, frogs, and snails.

Muskrats can eat so many marsh plants that they alter the nature of their own environment, changing the ratio of open water to dense vegetation. This generally enhances the habitat's value for marsh birds and waterfowl, increasing biological diversity.

Although they are much smaller than a beaver—another aquatic mammal that can have an out-sized impact on its environment— muskrats are large for a rodent. Adults weigh about 2 pounds and measure roughly 20 inches from the tip of the nose to the end of the 10-inch tail. They make tempting meals for maraud-ing predators such as mink,

fox, and weasel. Bald eagles and other birds of prey can eat so many muskrats that they influence the size of the population over time. When swimming, muskrats can fall victim to large northern pike, pickerel, and snapping turtles. To survive this onslaught, muskrats are mostly active at night and during the hours of dawn and dusk.

Wintering muskrats that venture out onto the snow leave long-fingered, hand-like tracks that look like half-sized raccoon paw prints, but with a sinuous line in between them, left by the dragging tail. Front paws leave four-fingered tracks, while the rear tracks show five toes.

Winter can be treacherous both above and below the ice. Paul Errington, the renowned hunter, trapper, and wildlife biologist, recorded some dramatic moments in muskrat lives in his landmark book, *Of Men and Marshes*, including this scene one winter morning: "The whole top of the lodge shell is open, empty of muskrats, and powdered by the trace of snow. A mink-killed muskrat lies smeared with blood on the ice, and a drag trail represents another victim."

Half of a muskrat population can die by midwinter. During cold snaps, the openings to their winter lodges sometimes freeze shut, closing off access to oxygen and nourishment. As winter progresses, competition for food intensifies, forcing some muskrats to venture out into the open, where they can succumb to cold or fall prey to a coyote, fisher, dog, or a hunter's trap. Fortunately, the prolific muskrat is the most abundant fur-bearing animal in North America, producing two to three litters each year.

When spring finally arrives, the muskrat winter camps collapse during ice-out. By then muskrats are traveling about on land, where the males deposit a pungent scent along their routes, marking their territories for the start of the mating season. This oily "musk" exudes from a gland at the base of the muskrat's tail.

By early spring, the adults have kicked the previous autumn's youngsters out of the house. In April or May, about a month after mating, new litters are born. Each consists of from three to nine naked, hairless kits that are about 4 inches long. Around midsummer, the adolescent muskrats are driven away to make room for a second litter. By the time ice-fishing shacks reappear, adult muskrats, along with the late-summer crop of young, will again be hunkered down in their own winter homes and shanties.

# Biding Time

## WINTER SEEDS AND BUDS

WHEN SNOW FINALLY ARRIVED this winter, and high winds followed, I knew the trees would be on the move. Not just dancing in the breeze, but spreading into new territory. Many of our native species drop small, lightweight seeds that are blown great distances over the surface of the snow.

Seeds of birches—white, yellow, gray, and black or "sweet" birch—are familiar to those who walk the winter woods. Up to one thousand seeds are attached to each tight seed cluster, or *catkin*. Seeds are enclosed in tiny scales that resemble a *fleur-de-lis*, or "iris blossom," an iconic image that dates back to ancient Mesopotamia. When cold weather intensifies, scales detach from the center spike of the catkin in an ascending spiral. As the scales flit over the snow, the smaller, winged seeds chafe off and sail even farther. Winter-drop seeds have the highest rates of germination among birches. When windblown seeds collect in the lee of a snowdrift, they sometimes sprout a line of seedlings come springtime.

This form of seed dispersal is so successful that many of our native trees deliberately drop seeds in winter, including such cone-bearing species as pitch pine, hemlock, and larch. I often find seeds of hophornbeam atop the snow amid those of hemlock—two trees that tend to associate in our forests. Down in the wet places, the cone-like seeds of alder drop near beaver lodges, and each seed ball of the riparian sycamore releases two hundred or more parasoled wings to ride the chill breath of Old Man Winter.

Wherever they land, many seeds require extended exposure to the cold in order to sprout come springtime. During the late summer, sugar maple seeds

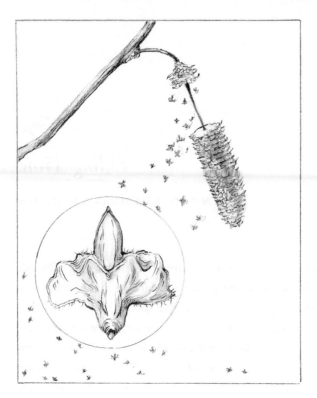

*Birch catkin shedding scales and seeds.*

spin away from the tree on whirligigs called *samaras*. Once they land, they must experience up to six months of winter cold before becoming ready to sprout. No cold, no baby sugar maples.

The seeds of many beloved wildflowers also lie in wait for the life-bringing kiss of cold, including those of baneberry, vervain, betony, hellebore, jack-in-the-pulpit, and wild rose. Members of the diverse crowfoot family—such as columbine, hepatica, anemone, monkshood, marsh marigold (cowslip), and buttercup—produce seeds that will not germinate unless they've experienced prolonged temperatures between 15 and 25 degrees Fahrenheit.

Why do many seeds need to experience the winter cold before they can germinate? It comes down to basic survival. If every seed sprouted at the flush of our first February thaw, or during a prolonged, languid autumn, then tender seedlings would risk being killed as soon as the cold weather returned. In order to prevent this from happening, seeds and buds enter a state of dormancy, a word that comes from the Latin *dormire*, "to sleep."

Dormancy begins when days grow short, sunlight becomes less intense, and temperatures drop. Sugars, minerals, and proteins move out of the leaves and into winter storage in roots, trunks, and branches. Leaves fall from twigs, where buds have already formed. Each bud contains an embryonic leaf or flower enclosed in protective scales that help to keep it from drying out or freezing.

Dormant buds have everything they need to grow into leaves and flowers, but hormones called *dormins* repress their growth and induce a state of rest. One plant hormone, abscisic acid, particularly inhibits buds and seeds. Some seeds, like acorns and walnuts, also have a thick, hard coat that shields them from winter weather.

Even if the weather warms up in midwinter, most dormant seeds and buds will not start growing. Dormancy will only break when the days grow longer and warmer, the rain returns, and soil thaws so roots can again absorb water and minerals. Then the plant's growth chemicals, such as ethylene, begin to encourage roots, stems, and buds to grow.

The system doesn't always work perfectly. A late-arriving winter on the heels of a mild autumn may prompt some buds to break dormancy and start to unfurl prematurely. During the unusually warm extended autumn of 2007, some cherry trees in Washington, D.C., blossomed in early December, as did apple orchards and vineyards in Europe. Once this happens, delicate plant tissues lie open and exposed to the wrath of the returning winter, and they stand little chance of surviving. Even buds that haven't actually opened may already have broken dormancy; these will freeze inside when winter returns.

For the plants that have adapted to our temperate climate, dormancy usually doesn't release its hold until they have been exposed to sufficient cold weather, long enough to have made it safely into the warm vernal days. For example, a lilac bush placed in a warm greenhouse all winter will not form leaves or flowers come springtime. But if a single branch on the same lilac protrudes through a hole in the glass and is exposed to the cold, it will sprout leaves and bloom. This proves, beyond doubt, that the North Country's springtime riot of green foliage and rainbow blossoms requires a steady diet of cold, hard winter.

# How Birds of a Feather Survive Winter Nights

SOME WINTERS PAST, a pair of Carolina wrens frequented our bird feeder. The male greeted the dawn with an ebullient "tea-kettle, tea-kettle, tea-kettle." After sunset, the intrepid wrens retired to the warmth and safety of our barn. Early each day, as I opened the barn door and bid them "good morning," I was reminded of a friend and farmer who once had an eastern towhee, another bird not common to the season, overwinter in his barn in Barnard, Vermont. The resourceful towhee roosted in a warm corner of the barn, near the animals, and helped itself to some of their grain.

Barns aside, friends who enjoy the winter birds at our feeder often ask how any bird could possibly survive the sub-zero nights. Answer: they take advantage of the shelter and insulation provided by thick evergreens and dense shrubs; these are the most common nocturnal winter roosts for many birds. One of our more popular bird feeders hangs near a row of bushy white pines. Come sunset, blue jays, juncos, mourning doves, and cardinals fly into these pines and settle for the night, somewhat protected from cold winds, snow, or rain.

Birds also spend winter nights under peeling bark on tree trunks, in vines that cover buildings, and under eaves. Purple finches roost en masse in pines and hemlocks. Birds that nest in cavities during breeding season often use tree hollows for winter shelter; these include chickadees, titmice, nuthatches, bluebirds, screech owls, and both downy and hairy woodpeckers.

Wintering white-breasted nuthatches pool their body heat by huddling in groups of up to two dozen. Turkeys and crows employ the same survival strategy, often flocking in evergreen treetops, the latter congregating in groups of as many as several thousand. Crows return to the same roost each night from as far as twenty miles away.

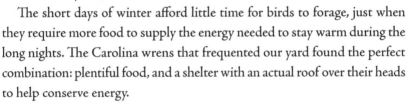

*Carolina Wren*

Not all birds take to the trees for protection. The ruffed grouse, for example, digs under snow or dive-bombs into a snowbank to hollow out a tunnel. Within this warmer shelter, grouse might expend roughly half the energy they would need in the open air. Grouse also have downy plumes that branch from their main feathers, a nice coat to wear while surrounded by snow.

The short days of winter afford little time for birds to forage, just when they require more food to supply the energy needed to stay warm during the long nights. The Carolina wrens that frequented our yard found the perfect combination: plentiful food, and a shelter with an actual roof over their heads to help conserve energy.

In his book, *Life in the Cold*, the renowned field biologist and winter ecologist Peter Marchand observes that most winter songbirds run on a tight energy budget, possessing just enough fat reserves to survive one extremely cold winter night. So it is critical that they retain as much heat as possible in order to keep their body temperatures within the necessary range of 104 to 109 degrees Fahrenheit. Most birds grow a thicker coat of insulating feathers as winter approaches. The winter coats of goldfinches and redpolls, for example, weigh one and a half times their summer plumage. Birds can also increase insulation by 50 percent simply by fluffing up their feathers. In extreme cold, birds will tuck in their necks, legs, and wings to avoid losing heat from these extremities. Scientists have found that if birds reduce their exposed surface area by one-fourth, then heat loss decreases by an equal amount. To save even more energy, chickadees can lower their nocturnal body temperature by 10 to 12 degrees.

These and other heat-conservation techniques usually work, but when they prove inadequate, birds have yet another strategy at their disposal: shivering. Birds shiver constantly to generate body heat. According to Marchand, shivering goldfinches can increase their typical heat output fivefold when exposed to very cold temperatures.

Besides shivering, birds have an internal heat exchange system that helps maintain their core temperature. As warm arterial blood is pumped toward the cold feet, that blood comes into close contact with the cooler blood returning through the veins to the heart. This near-contact warms the venous blood so that it doesn't unduly chill the body core.

As well equipped as birds are for surviving winter nights, there are ways we humans can help. Create sheltering brush piles in the woods, leave dead trees standing for the birds that roost in cavities, and cut small access holes in sheds for winter birds seeking shelter. Come spring, consider planting thick evergreens for winter cover and put in a few berry-bearing shrubs to provide cold-weather food.

And finally, don't forget to leave that barn door open, by just a feather, for the wrens and towhees.

# HABITATS

# The Great Pond Adventure

PONDS ARE PLACES OF ENDLESS DISCOVERIES. They are liquid eyes gazing up to the sky and catching the sun's life-giving energy. Who wouldn't want to spend a summer day at the pond?

The next time you head to a pond for a cool dip on a hot day, turn your trip into an adventure. Bring a shallow white tray with sides high enough to hold water, a pair of tweezers, a large strainer, a hand lens, and some old sneakers for mucking around. Take along a copy of an easy-to-use field guide such as *Pond Life* by George K. Reid.

Find a shallow pond with a safe, gradual slope along the shore. (Water wings are always a good idea for young children.) Fill the tray with clear water and place it in the shade at the water's edge. As you wade in the shallows, sift the strainer through the plants and mud and you'll catch globs of muck crawling with insects, worms, and other forms of aquatic life. Use the tweezers to gently lift each critter out of the strainer, taking a close look through the hand lens. Then place each one into the tray of water.

While you're mucking about, be careful not to slip on the mats of algae. Although individual algae are very small, as sun-catchers they are the major source of energy that feeds the animals in the pond's food chain. Algae are as important to the pond as a field of grass is to a herd of grazing cows.

Most ponds are full of microscopic crustaceans that eat free-floating algae, but the side-swimmer, or scud, is large enough to see. It looks like a tiny shrimp doing the sidestroke as it searches for dead plants and animals to eat. Its larger relative, the crayfish, is also a scavenger.

Mosquito larvae rest at the surface with breathing tubes exposed to the air like snorkels. Phantom midge larvae have flotation devices that look like tiny water wings. These and other larvae are eaten by young fish, water striders, whirligig beetles, and fish spiders.

Water striders use the water's surface much as a spider uses its web to catch prey, locating their food by sensing vibrations in the surface film. When a fly, moth, or some other insect gets caught, the strider skates over and uses piercing-sucking mouthparts to finish off its meal.

Whirligig beetles are the shiny, bluish-black insects that gyrate around on top of the pond. Their eyes are divided horizontally into two parts, so that they can focus both in the air and underwater. When they dive, they use an air bubble as a tiny scuba tank.

If you catch an oblong insect that is covered in dark green algae, it is probably a predaceous dragonfly nymph. (Be careful, they can bite.) Tap the hind end of the nymph with the tweezers and it will shoot forward using jet propulsion, forcing water out the tip of its abdomen. These nymphs will eventually crawl to the edge of the pond, shed their skins, and spread gossamer dragonfly wings. Watch for adult dragonflies patrolling the air over the pond in search of prey. These aerial acrobats can hover in place or fly at up to 35 miles per hour—about the speed of a racehorse!

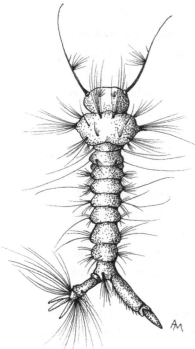

*Mosquito larva.*

When it comes to predators, a dragonfly nymph more than meets its match in a giant water bug. These flattish, oval insects ambush other insects, crustaceans, tadpoles, and even small frogs, then inject enzymes into their prey and suck up the innards. They can grow to be 3 inches long and pack a nasty bite that has earned them the nickname of "toe biter." The female giant water bug of the genus *Belostoma* lays and cements one hundred or more eggs onto the male's back. He dutifully carries the eggs for about a week until they hatch, and then protects the young nymphs from predators. Giant water bugs can also fly and

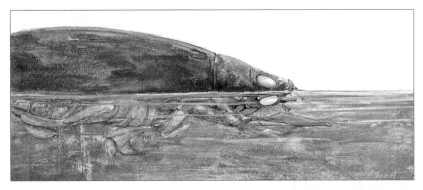

*Whirligig beetle.*

are sometimes called "electric light bugs" after their habit of buzzing around porch lights and streetlights. When handled, they squeak and emit a scent evocative of apples.

Moving up the food chain, the smaller predators are eaten by larger hunters like red-spotted newts, bluegill sunfish, catfish, and largemouth bass. Common water snakes, otters, and minks are among the pond's top predators. Swallows skim over the pond in search of insect meals, and I once watched a belted kingfisher swoop down to catch a dozen small fish during the course of an hour.

As the sun begins to set, watch for the fluttery flight of bats above the pond. Bats eat more than their own weight in mosquitoes and other insects each night.

When your adventure at the pond is over and it's time to leave, gently release everything you've caught into shallow water. Taking care of life in the pond means that there will be no end to the mysteries that await the next visitor.

# Breathing New Life
# into Old Fields

THERE IS MAGIC in an old field. Butterflies flutter, crickets call, meadow voles scurry through matted grasses, and black-and-yellow garden spiders ambush from dew-spangled webs. Early June footsteps release the floral sweetness of wild strawberries. With heads in the sun, feet cooled by shade, ears full of insect songs, and noses imbued with the scents of wild herbs—an old field is our sensory garden. We loom over this waist-high world as a giant among the wildflowers.

But old fields are ever-changing, and nature wastes no opportunities. Fields that are no longer being hayed or pastured regularly become populated with a tangle of plants and, eventually, the beginnings of a forest. Because they are such mutable environments, these old fields disappear if not maintained and are among the least-common habitats in New England. In the mid-1800s, when farming in New England was at its peak, nearly four out of every five acres of land had been cleared. Over time, as agriculture declined, this trend reversed until trees now cover 80 percent of the landscape. In recent decades, old fields have become scarce.

Native and introduced species of plants quickly populate old fields. Planted timothy, alfalfa, and orchard grass become interspersed with sedges and the wild grasses of foxtail, little bluestem and, in wet places, reed canary grass. Seeds arrive via parasols, burrs, springs, catapults, and glider-like wings. Apple trees, wild cherries, and other fruit-bearers wrap seeds inside tasty flesh so that they will be deposited wherever birds, deer, and other frugivores leave droppings.

Ox-eye daisy, toadflax (butter-and-eggs), and the yellow pea-like bird's-foot trefoil are among the early bloomers. Midsummer blossoms include black-eyed Susan, milkweed, cinquefoil, and Queen Anne's lace. Late summer and early autumn come alive with the rich hues of goldenrods, the bright rays of asters, and the down of thistle seeds, a staple food for American goldfinches. My favorite is the tiny white flower of old-field balsam, also known as fragrant everlasting, whose autumn scent evokes calico and old lace.

Insects are drawn to these farms gone wild. Grasshoppers and crickets sing from the greenery. Leafhoppers, or "spittle bugs," exude foamy white shelters. June's eastern black swallowtails are followed by the monarchs of July and August that famously lay eggs on milkweed. Flower spiders ambush pollinating insects with a toxic bite. These pale arachnids slowly color-shift to match white or yellow flowers.

About 40 percent of eastern wildlife species—from red foxes and white-tailed deer to eastern coyotes, woodchucks, cottontails, and short-tailed shrews—rely on old-field habitats at some stage of their lives. Weasels and garter snakes hunt here for the ubiquitous mice and meadow voles.

Ironically, old-field plants create conditions less suitable for their own progeny by providing deeper shade, taller shrubs, greater soil moisture, moderated temperature swings, and protection from the elements. Because these conditions are beneficial for those species that follow in their wake, annuals and perennials eventually yield to the shrubs and trees of a young forest. Raspberries and blackberries appear, along with sumac and sun-loving trees such as aspen, white pine, and black cherry. Wet meadows sport pussy willow, highbush blueberry, alder, and elderberry. Over time—barring fire, disease, or some other disturbance—a succession of ecological changes transforms open land into mature forest.

As the plants come and go, so do the animals. When grassland matures into an old field, eastern meadowlarks and bobolinks give way to melodious song sparrows and field sparrows whose voices recall the quickening beats of a bouncing ping-pong ball. In early springtime, American woodcocks launch aerial displays from hedgerows. Damp, shrub-studded fields attract the vociferous common yellowthroat and the rapidly disappearing golden-winged warbler.

Well-planned and timely cuttings are needed to create or maintain diverse

old-field habitats. Years ago, when I was land manager for the Audubon Society of Rhode Island, I maintained fields in the various nature preserves with regular cuttings. As a novice mower, I would circle fields and cut in toward the center. But I soon discovered that this technique herded everything from crickets to voles into the ever-shrinking, uncut portion until, with the last pass of the singing blades, I became Jack the Reaper. So I learned to divide fields into sections and mow back and forth along one edge, driving animals into the safety of sections that had already been cut instead of corralling them in the middle.

I aimed to mow each section once every four to five years, on a rotating schedule, to maintain varied stages of growth. My sections were about a quarter-acre in size, and I mowed in late August, when the young of ground-nesting birds had fledged. Mowing in curves, scallops, and other irregular shapes creates longer edges between sections of varying ages, which increases diversity and enhances the field's value as wildlife habitat. I also maintained a few small islands of shrubs and tall trees where birds of prey, such as red-tailed hawks, could perch, kestrels could nest, and other animals find shade.

I mowed every year in areas wherever invasive species such as Japanese honeysuckle, common buckthorn, and glossy buckthorn appeared. These fast-growing species can be eradicated only if the mowing is done regularly.

The effort required to maintain old fields is well rewarded. When wind forms waves of grasses and blossoms, we are as sailors scanning the swells in a sea of flowers. We are Gullivers in this colorful land of Lilliput—witnessing the minute mysteries of a knee-deep ecosystem.

# Remarkable Riparians

TO WILDLIFE BIOLOGISTS, the benefits of maintaining healthy "riparian buffers" are self-evident. But to most people, these terms are obscure. *Riparian* comes from the Latin *riparius*, meaning "bank." The shores of rivers, streams, and lakes are critical boundaries between uplands and open water. Steep riparian habitats may be only 50 to 100 feet wide, but gently sloping shores along broad lakes and meandering rivers are lined with intermittently flooded meadows, swamps, and bogs that can span thousands of feet.

These ecological transition zones form essential habitat for plants and animals, providing food, cover, and water, along with places for resting, breeding, and raising young. In addition to harboring beaver, mink, muskrat, otter, heron, woodcock, loon, yellow warbler, wood duck, osprey, and others, riparian habitats support an array of plants useful to humans and wildlife alike, including red and silver maple, green ash, willow, alder, blueberry, cranberry, elderberry, groundnut, boneset, cattail, Joe-Pye weed, and arrowhead.

During spring melting and periods of heavy rain, the plants and soils of riparian wetlands store excess runoff, which then flows slowly into surrounding waters. This curtails flooding overall, allows silt to settle before entering waterways, and decreases peak flood levels. It also curtails scouring from water and ice along riverbanks. From 50 to 100 percent of sediment settles out and is filtered as runoff passes through the riparian zone. When water meanders through wetlands, it also percolates and recharges groundwater.

Riparian environments act as shields or *buffers* that protect bodies of water from shoreline disturbances. Soil particles, plant litter, roots, and bacteria absorb 80 to 90 percent of nutrient runoff and pesticides before these enter

*Riparian buffers.*

surface waters and aquifers. Plant roots form mats that bind the soil in place and prevent erosion.

Overhanging branches cast shade that is essential for trout and other cool-water species. Autumn leaves provide food energy for aquatic insects. Fallen tree trunks and branches create habitats for insects, trout, and other wildlife. Flowing water is churned up by these obstacles and enriched with oxygen.

Riparian environments perch precariously between humankind and aquatic ecosystems and are easily disturbed or destroyed. Forestry and construction projects that remove all of the trees can cause shorelines to slump. Plowing up to the water's edge or grazing animals along the banks can create erosion. Such impacts are compounded when runoff carries nutrients from manure and fertilizers plus toxins from pesticides. Mowing lawns down to the shoreline both eliminates habitat and allows lawn chemicals to flow directly into the water.

These activities enable waves and currents to remove soil from lakeshores and riverbanks. Silt can bury the gravels of spawning grounds, envelop fish eggs, and coat the gills of fish and aquatic insects, causing stress and suffoca-

*Dead-tree fish habitat.*

tion. When shade from overhanging vegetation is removed, water heats up and holds less dissolved oxygen. This creates unfavorable conditions for trout and salmon as well as their favorite foods, such as stoneflies. Nutrients that enter waterways from eroded soil and fertilizer runoff promote algal blooms, whose decay can further deplete the supply of oxygen.

Destroying riparian buffers also takes an economic toll. Streams and rivers that flow through denuded shorelines remove tons of soil. Over time, stream channels can wash away acres of valuable farmland. Floodwaters rise faster and crest higher—inundating properties downstream and undermining roads and bridge abutments.

What can be done? The solution is simple—*laissez faire*. Wherever shoreline vegetation already exists, nature will do its job if we just let it be. The Connecticut River Watershed Council recommends maintaining buffers 50 feet wide to stabilize gradual slopes (100 feet for steep banks); 100 feet wide to protect fish habitat and filter nutrient runoff and pesticides; 150 feet wide to control erosion and sediments; 200 feet wide to mitigate flooding; and 300 to 600 feet wide for optimal wildlife habitat.

Fences can exclude livestock from riparian habitats. During forestry operations, erosion can be minimized by limiting stream crossings and using staked hay bales and silt fences. If a shoreline property has eroded and its habitat degraded, the banks can be stabilized and buffers restored with native plants.

Landowners can find advice, technical expertise, and financial assistance for protecting and improving critical riparian habitat and for creating a wise, long-term land management plan. Several programs are available through the U.S. Department of Agriculture, including the Conservation Stewardship Program, Environmental Quality Incentive Program, Agricultural Management Assistance, and the Forest Service's National Best Management Practices (BMP) Program. The U.S. Fish and Wildlife Service runs the Partners for Fish and Wildlife Program.

In addition to their environmental and economic virtues, riparian habitats are prime areas for fishing, boating, swimming, bird watching, and nature photography. They also are crucial environments for educational programs and scientific study. And they are of inestimable value for reconnecting with nature and our aesthetic enjoyment of the outdoors.

# For Peat's Sake

IN 1848, workers constructing the railroad line from Bellows Falls to Rutland, Vermont, found the remains of a mastodon buried 11 feet deep in a Mount Holly bog. One tusk was nearly 8 feet long. Seventeen years later, farmhands working a peat bog in Brattleboro struck part of a mastodon tusk that measured 4 feet long and 18 inches around. It is still on display as a "mammoth tusk" in Brattleboro's Brooks Memorial Library.

How can Ice Age relics survive in peat bogs? Saturated with water, deprived of oxygen, and highly acidic (due to the influence of *Sphagnum* moss), peat mats inhibit the decomposing actions of bacteria and fungi. Some prehistoric tree trunks have remained so intact in bogs that they can still be used for fuel or lumber. Ancient bogs can therefore act as biological time capsules, preserving pollen, seeds, spores, woody plants, and even animals.

Scandinavian bogs have produced a macabre crop—the undecomposed bodies of Iron Age people who were killed and thrown into the mire, as described in *The Bog People* by P. V. Glob. The remains of one man discovered in a Danish bog in 1950 still sported a five-o'clock shadow, even though he had been sacrificed 2,000 years ago to the fertility goddess *Nerthus*, "Mother Earth."

Because so little decomposition occurs in peat bogs, nutrients can be scarce. Some bog plants supplement their nutrition by capturing animal food with ingenious mechanisms, including our native sundews (sticky hairs), pitcher plants (drowning pools), and bladderworts (tiny aquatic vacuum cleaners). (Charles W. Johnson's *Bogs of the Northeast* describes these fascinating carnivorous plants.)

*Sphagnum* moss has been used by humans for millennia. The Abenaki peoples of northern New England used it for diapers, poultices, and insulation. Colonists stuffed pillows and mattresses with it. In Finland, Ireland, Russia, and Belarus, people burn blocks of dried peat to generate both heat and electricity.

Today, peat moss is also used as a growth medium for seeds and seedlings, as a soil amendment, and to make peat pots. The world's leading sources of horticultural peat are Canada, Germany, Estonia, the United Kingdom, Finland, and Ireland. The United States buys 90 percent of Canada's peat exports, largely from Quebec and New Brunswick.

Like rainforests, peatlands are expansive ecosystems that face numerous threats. Countless peatlands have been drained for agriculture, while others have been denuded of the peat itself. Removing peat destroys the habitat and is akin to strip-mining. First, the bog is drained of water by ditching. Then the surface vegetation is stripped away, and the upper layer of peat is "milled" or turned up with a harrow. After drying in the sun for several days, the peat is vacuumed up, screened, packed, and shipped.

Far more than a precious ecosystem is lost when peat is harvested. Peatlands are thought to contain greater reservoirs of carbon than all of the world's rainforests combined. The anaerobic bacteria in peatlands produce methane, a greenhouse gas twenty times more potent than carbon dioxide. In an intact bog, the overlying layer of plants traps the methane in such quantity that the bog mat may inflate up to eight inches. Normally, this methane slowly escapes into the atmosphere; peat mining releases the methane all at once. When peat is burned or used for horticulture, that carbon also enters the atmosphere and contributes to global warming. In cold regions, the peat layer insulates the permafrost beneath; when the peat is removed, the frozen ground melts and decays, releasing still more carbon.

Naturally growing peat accumulates at the rate of 8 to 32 inches every 1,000 years. The

*Pitcher plant.*

5- to 6-foot drainage ditches made during mining can remove bottom layers that are 9,000 years old—laid down only a thousand years after the bellow of the last mastodon echoed across the land. Still, the peat industry refers to the harvest of peat as sustainable. Although Canadian law mandates that post-production peatlands be restored to "working wetlands," the peat itself can only regenerate at a millennial pace.

Fortunately, there are excellent alternatives to horticultural peat moss. Coir (pronounced "koy'-er"), or "coco peat" is an organic, renewable byproduct made from coconut husks. Coir fibers can be used to make mats, ropes, and other goods. The waste husks are composted to create potting soil, soil conditioner, fiber pots, and a hydroponic growth medium. Coir adds organic matter to soil, which improves tilth and aeration. It increases drainage in compacted soils and water retention in porous media. Coir pots can be planted because they decompose. Marketed as "Crop Circles," dehydrated disks of coir can swell to five times their original volume when water is added.

Pine bark mulch is another good alternative for starting seeds and seedlings. Composted bark mulch makes a fertile soil supplement and contains few pathogens.

A company named Organix composts manure anaerobically, in a sealed environment, which decreases the amount of methane released into the atmosphere, reduces groundwater contamination, and minimizes the nutrients that enter waterways. The methane generated is captured for fuel. The resulting odorless solids, sold as "RePeet," can be used for horticulture and to make planting pots.

Still, there's no substitute for the cheapest, most widely available, and most environmentally friendly alternative to peat moss: homegrown, composted kitchen and garden waste.

# The Pond in Winter

IN THE SPRING OF 1984, while writing *Pond and Brook*, I spent several months working on the top floor of Dartmouth College's Baker Library. One day, while walking past nearby Occom Pond, I was stunned to see the ice melting and the shore littered with hundreds of fish—bloated, sallow bodies sporting eyes clouded with death. Over the next few days I was repeatedly asked, "What killed all of those fish at Occom Pond?"

"In some winters, the oxygen level in the water becomes so low that fish can suffocate," I replied.

"But why doesn't that happen every year?" came the inevitable follow-up.

So I had to get technical: When a pond freezes over, it becomes sealed off from the normal exchange of gases between air and water. Oxygen above the ice cannot mix with the water, while carbon dioxide from the respiration of animals becomes trapped below. Meanwhile, gases released by decomposers accumulate near the bottom of the pond, including carbon dioxide, hydrogen sulfide, and ammonia.

Some aquatic plants, algae, and other life-forms continue to use whatever sunlight passes through the ice for photosynthesis, releasing oxygen and absorbing carbon dioxide in the process. But as the ice thickens and becomes covered with snow, less light penetrates and less oxygen is produced. Winter's shorter days and colder temperatures also decrease the amount of oxygen being generated in the sunlight-starved pond. For example, a submerged plant called Canadian waterweed (*Elodea canadensis*) typically produces only half the oxygen in winter that it does during midsummer.

In short, when ice forms early in the winter, is covered with snow, and stays late, oxygen levels can fall so drastically, especially in shallow ponds, that fish begin to die off.

Paradoxically, the coating of ice also protects pond life from the extremes of winter weather. Although some plants and insects overwinter as dormant seeds or eggs, much pond life continues on as usual throughout the winter, though at a slower pace that requires less food and oxygen. The temperature of water under the ice, and that of the cold-blooded animals that live there, hovers just above freezing. In *Life in the Cold*, Peter Marchand observes that, for every 10-degree Celsius drop in water temperature, a cold-blooded animal's metabolic rate is cut in half.

Minnows remain sluggishly active, as do red-spotted newts, tadpoles, and crayfish. Free-swimming carnivorous insects are on the prowl, including whirligig beetles, predaceous diving beetles, and the aquatic bugs called backswimmers. These insects employ tiny bubbles and silvery films of air as minute aqualungs into which oxygen diffuses from the surrounding water.

Cut a hole in the ice, scoop up some mud, and you'll catch the same, gill-equipped immature stages of insects that you would find in summer, including mayflies, caddisflies, dragonflies, and damselflies. As the mud along the edge of the pond freezes deeper, many insects continue burrowing down. Some, such as mayflies and caddisflies, can even survive freezing.

Muskrats huddle in dome-shaped winter lodges of mud-packed cattails, plunging often into the icy water to search for food. In winter, the level of oxygen-carrying hemoglobin in their blood increases, enabling longer dives under the ice for foraging on submerged stems and roots. Beavers snuggle to preserve body heat. When hungry, they leave the lodge by an underwater entryway and swim a short distance to their winter cache of branches, which they cut and push into the mud during the fall. These robust aquatic rodents also rely on autumn stores of body fat to survive. In winter, a diving beaver's pulse rate drops so low that it can remain submerged for fifteen minutes.

Cold-blooded animals take this strategy to the extreme, dramatically decreasing their heartbeat, circulation, metabolism, and growth. Bluegills, for example, can enter a state of suspended animation while remaining buoyant. Garter snakes sometimes hibernate in crayfish burrows at the pond's edge. Snakes occasionally share the same hibernacula with frogs and salamanders—animals which, in autumn, might have been the snake's erstwhile prey.

*Predaceous diving beetle.*

Snapping turtles and painted turtles also hibernate near the edge of the pond, tucking into a winter bed of mud.

Despite numerous studies, scientists have yet to discover exactly how the normally air-breathing turtle survives being submerged all winter in oxygen-challenged conditions. Dormant turtles may absorb some oxygen directly through the surface of their exposed skin. As lactic acid accumulates in their bloodstream, due to respiration in an oxygen-poor environment, chemical buffers—calcium, magnesium and potassium—become more concentrated, neutralizing the acid.

Turtles will occasionally awaken under the ice. I recall the frigid, snowless early winter of 1975, when a thick layer of clear "black" ice formed over the ponds. During a late-December walk along the trails of the Caratunk Wildlife Refuge in Seekonk, Massachusetts, I ventured out onto the ice where, eerily suspended above the living diorama, I saw a spotted turtle swim lazily by. That window into another world, that clear crystalline floor beneath my feet, was the turtle's winter sky.

WATER &
WETLANDS

# The Comeback Canary

OUR COMMON LOON

PRIMAL, ELEMENTAL, AND EVOCATIVE of the wild recesses of the human spirit, the "common" loon is among our most beloved birds. Fossils that look very similar to modern-day loons date back 22 million years. Genetic sleuthing has revealed that loons are related to several groups of birds, including penguins and the "tube-nosed swimmers" such as albatrosses, petrels, and shearwaters.

These strikingly beautiful creatures have bones denser than those of other flying birds, enabling them to dive deeply underwater. A sort of avian 747, their size and weight requires them to flap and pad across the water's surface for up to a quarter of a mile before liftoff. If they land on small ponds, they can't get airborne again.

After overwintering on the open sea, loons return to breed in northern New England and central Massachusetts in April and May. En route, they fly up to 75 miles per hour. Loons that have successfully nested tend to come back to the same nesting ground the following year. Once they return, they usually pair with the same partner to construct a nest of mud, soggy plants, and moss, 2 feet across and 6 inches above the water level. Because a loon's feet are so far back that it must push along on land, nests must be close to the water's edge.

The female usually lays two eggs in the nest. In about 27 days, the chicks hatch. They enter the water as soon as their down is dry, encouraged by soft calls from their parents. Hungry chicks use a shrill begging call. Parents sing a duet to defend the breeding grounds. The most famous loon songs are

the long, haunting wail that loons use to locate one another, along with the tremolo, which loons use either to signal their presence or a sense of alarm.

Parents feed the chicks aquatic insects, small fish, and crayfish. On the hunt, adults ply the waters with powerful hind feet at depths of up to 200 feet. A typical dive lasts for about a minute, but they can submerge for up to three minutes and only need to stick their bill up for air before diving again. Young loons begin to molt into adult plumage at just over two years of age. On average, loons begin to breed and reproduce at about six years old.

New England's loon populations were once in dire straits. According to Harry Vogel, senior biologist and executive director of the Loon Preservation Committee in Moultonborough, New Hampshire, there were 74 pairs of nesting loons statewide back in 1976. A mere 48 chicks hatched that year, and 44 of them survived into autumn. Eric Hanson, project biologist for the Vermont Loon Conservation Project of the Vermont Center for Ecostudies, said that a scant 7 nesting pairs produced just 9 surviving chicks in 1983. (Vermont overall has less suitable breeding habitat than New Hampshire.)

Extensive research and intensive management have helped loon populations to steadily recover. Preservation efforts include monitoring and protecting prime breeding grounds, creating artificial nest platforms, stabilizing water levels, educating the public, and posting warning signs in breeding areas.

In 2021, there were 229 nesting pairs in New Hampshire; 133 chicks survived to the end of the breeding season. New Hampshire's loons are found mostly in the North Country and Lakes Region; they are absent from the higher White Mountains and uncommon in the south. The Northeast Kingdom is home to some 85 percent of Vermont's loon population of 109 nesting pairs (2021), which produced 84 surviving chicks. Nests also can be found amid the lakes and reservoirs of the central and southern Green Mountains. Maine is loon central for New England—with a summer population of some 1700 breeding pairs producing 224 chicks in the southern half of the state alone.

But these iconic birds still face a multitude of threats. People disturb them on their nesting and feeding grounds. Construction destroys habitat. Changes in water levels either strand or flood nests. Waves from passing boats wash eggs away. Loons are sometimes shot, run over by boats, or tangled in fishing line. Oil spills are a hazard where they overwinter in the ocean. Many loons die when they ingest lead sinkers or lead-headed fishing jigs attached to broken and discarded fishing lines, as well as lead tackle found along lake bottoms. Long-term, region-wide studies have found that nearly half of all breeding adult loons found dead or dying in New England each year are the victims of confirmed or suspected lead poisoning.

Loons are the proverbial canaries in the coal mine. Many toxins found in our environment can build up (*bioaccumulate*) in an animal's tissues over time and become more concentrated (*biomagnify*) farther up the food web. As long-lived predators, perched at the top of aquatic food webs, loons are excellent indicators of environmental problems.

Loons are especially affected by one particularly insidious environmental contaminant—the mercury that comes from airborne pollution created by coal-burning power plants, combustion engines, and incinerators. Roughly

half of all mercury contamination is from local and regional sources. By band-
ing and monitoring loons, researchers have observed changes in behavior and
reproductive success due to mercury contamination. Mercury causes abnormal
behavior in loon adults, making it harder for them to establish and defend
nesting territories. The survival of loon chicks is down by 40 percent in some
lakes where mercury levels are high. In the egg, a developing embryo can be
killed by mercury concentrations as low as 1.3 parts per million.

Reducing mercury contamination in the environment is a complex and
long-term issue (see "Heavy Metal Blues"), but lead poisoning in loons is an
easier problem to tackle. It is now illegal to use small lead tackle in Maine,
New Hampshire, Vermont, Massachusetts, New York, and several other
northern states, as well as Canadian national parks and national wildlife areas.

To help preserve these magnificent birds, contact the Loon Preservation
Committee (New Hampshire), the Vermont Loon Conservation Project at the
Vermont Center for Ecostudies, or the Center for Loon Conservation at the
Biodiversity Research Institute (Maine). Encourage friends and family to stop
using lead sinkers and jigs and ask local stores to carry only non-lead tackle.

It is rare that such simple actions can help to save a species in peril, but
Harry Vogel reminds us that the loon's comeback in the wild came about as a
result of intensive management. "More than ninety percent of the loons that
hatched in New Hampshire in 2015 benefited from our help, and we're not sure
they'll be able to persist in New Hampshire in the future without our help."

Because the loon in New England is close to its southern range, and loons nest at the edge of the water, climate change is also going to present challenges as temperatures rise and water levels fluctuate. According to Vogel, "The results of some preliminary analyses indicate that there is real cause for concern. Loons may become the avian poster-child for the effects of climate change in New England."

# Dragonflies and Damselflies

SOME YEARS AGO, while trekking near the summit of Mount Washington, I looked up toward the peak and saw a dragonfly silently glide by. What heights had it scaled before passing me? My tired limbs seemed all the more earthbound for that evanescent, six-legged biplane that appeared to have ridden a downdraft from the heights of some Olympus of the Insecta.

Dragonflies are nature's aeronautical marvels. Whether darting over water at 35 miles per hour or hovering in midair, they are a spectacle of colors in motion—from a delicate blue-green translucency to a jack-o'-lantern black and orange.

It's no surprise that dragonflies have entered the lore of many cultures over the ages. Henry David Thoreau once called them "devil's needles," though he certainly knew they were harmless. Centuries ago, Samurai warriors of Japan incorporated them into family crests, signifying victory over their enemies. Navajos of the American Southwest offer a more positive spin—they believe dragonflies to be a symbol of pure water.

The Dragonfly Society of the Americas recognizes 463 species of dragonflies and their close relatives, damselflies, living in North America; more than 180 of these species have been found in New England. Dragonflies and damselflies belong to the insect order *Odonata*, a name that comes from the Greek *odon*, meaning "tooth." The aquatic nymphs employ a hinged mouthpart that shoots out from under the head and grabs prey between two powerful pincers. Adults of both groups look similar in many ways, but dragonflies have thicker bodies, beat their wings twice as fast, and rest with their wings spread open. The more delicate damselflies typically rest with wings folded together over their back (except for the spread-winged damselflies).

In motion, damselflies personify grace and refinement, while dragonflies project power and precision. Dragonflies can hover, fly sideways and backward, mate on the wing, and turn 90 degrees on an aerial dime. They can move both pairs of wings independently and angle each wing to create various wind forces.

While adults are masters of the air, the eggs hatch into voracious aquatic nymphs or *naiads* that feed on other insects and virtually anything else small enough to swallow. One characteristic of dragonfly nymphs that helps them to hunt: their gills line a rectal chamber from which they can shoot water for a kind of jet propulsion. Damselfly nymphs have eyes on the sides of their heads and three feather-like gills at the end of the body that also help with swimming and positioning them in the water.

As nymphs, dragonflies and damselflies molt roughly a dozen times. Depending upon the species, the underwater stage may last from a couple of months to several years, with many pond species maturing in about a year. During the warm season, at night or in the early morning, the nymphs crawl up onto stems, rocks, mud, or leaves and squeeze out of a split in the skin on their backs. Then they pump up the wings hydraulically using *hemolymph*, the insect equivalent of blood. The wings are spread out to dry in the sun before the adult makes its first flight.

*Adult dragonfly
emerging.*

Emerging dragonflies and damselflies are especially vulnerable to disturbance, since it takes 30 minutes or more for their adult wings and bodies to form and harden. During this critical time, they need to crawl up beyond the water level. A natural shoreline strewn with logs, rocks, or plants is needed, or else the vulnerable young adults may be damaged by the smallest waves and wakes.

Once they take to the air, dragonflies can fly at nearly the speed of a racehorse and easily capture prey on the wing using their legs as a kind of net. When a dragonfly sights a potential meal, it turns its head and body, calculates a precise trajectory that anticipates the flight path of its prey, and often flies along a straight line directly to the point of interception. They consume many kinds of insects, including mosquitoes, so humans should bear them no malice.

Although adult dragonflies and damselflies can range far on the wing, the aquatic nymphs can live only in fresh water that meets their specific needs. The level of dissolved oxygen is critical. Still waters—especially ponds, marshes, and the vegetated shorelines of lakes—tend to contain low to medium levels of oxygen. The water of cool, fast-flowing streams that tumble over rocks and logs blends lots of oxygen into the water. Cooler water also holds more dissolved gas. (Think of how a bubbling cold soft drink loses its fizz and becomes "flat" as it warms up.)

Dragonfly nymphs are barometers of water quality, according to Steve Fiske, aquatic biologist/benthologist for the Vermont Department of Environmental Conservation. Because many species live in the same habitat for two to three years, monitoring nymph populations over time gives a good indication of whether a habitat has been "disturbed or polluted," he says.

Biologists rate aquatic insects on a scale of 0 to 10, based on the level of pollution they can tolerate. This scale helps researchers to determine water quality in a given area. Those associated with low numbers require cleaner water, while those higher on the scale are more pollution-tolerant—they can survive in water with less oxygen and moderate to high organic pollution. Excessive levels of nutrients from fertilizers or manure runoff can cause great blooms of algae. When these algae die, bacterial decomposers consume much of the available oxygen in the water.

Some of my favorite dragonflies and damselflies are those with clean-water

nymphs, such as the graceful ebony jewelwing, or black-winged damselfly (*Calopteryx maculata*), which performs a kind of flutter-dance in the air. Nymphs of the black-winged damselfly are found in cool, flowing streams that hold high oxygen levels.

If your backyard borders a river, watch for the eye-catching "dragonhunter" (*Hagenius brevistylus*), whose nymph also lives in clean waters. With green eyes and a jet-black body sporting yellow racing stripes on the thorax and scalloped yellow lines along the abdomen, it is the Ferrari among dragonflies. As advertised, this alpha anisopteran hunts down other dragonflies.

Nymphs of the dragonflies known as the slaty skimmer (*Libellula incesta*) and the common green darner (*Anax junius*) are among those that can be found in ponds, marshes, and lakeshores with fairly low levels of dissolved oxygen and moderate amounts of organic pollution. Adult male slaty skimmers are unmistakable, with a deep azure body and glossy black eyes. They defend territories with arching strikes along the margins of shrubby shorelines. At nearly 3 inches long, green darners are among our largest dragonflies. Male green darners have a bright blue abdomen, an emerald green thorax, and a bulls-eye marking on top of the head. Females have a reddish-brown abdomen.

Nymphs of three common species are pollution-tolerant—a damselfly called the familiar bluet (*Enallagma civile*) and two dragonflies, the common whitetail (*Libellula lydia*) and the twelve-spotted skimmer (*Libellula pulchella*). Displaying its stout, powder-blue abdomen with white spots down the sides and wings with prominent black bands, the adult male whitetail is striking— an anisopteran blue jay. Males mark their aerial turf over wetlands and scuffle along the edges of adjacent territories. Adult "twelve-spots" are among the easiest to identify, with a blue-gray abdomen and three black spots on each wing, starting with black on the tip and alternating with white down to the base. Like other odonates, this species often wanders away from water into nearby meadows and fields.

Many environmental groups use dragonfly and damselfly nymphs to monitor the ecological health of our waterways, such as the Connecticut River Watershed Council and the New Hampshire Dragonfly Survey—a project of the New Hampshire Audubon Society, New Hampshire Fish and Game, and UNH Cooperative Extension Service. The Vermont Center for Ecostudies, the Maine Damselfly and Dragonfly Survey, and many other conservation organizations and individuals throughout New England and North America, conduct field research on odonates and post results online at Odonata Central, which tracks and studies these alluring aerialists and also hosts the website of the Dragonfly Society of the Americas.

Dragonfly and damselfly researchers and aficionados are protective and passionate about these spectacular aeronautical acrobats and their fascinating nymphs—stalkers in the murky depths that bring light to our awareness of the world around us.

# Eels on a Slippery Slope

WHEN I WAS A TEENAGER, the group I hung out with spent most of its spare time angling for two things: girls and the elusive lunker bass. The grand plan for either one was much the same: choose the correct bait, use the best line, cast into a prolific pool, set the hook, and reel them in. We always dreamed of netting a "keeper" but, in reality, we were lucky just to get a nibble.

During one languid fishing trip to Worden's Pond in South Kingstown, Rhode Island, the end of my rod dipped into the water with such force that it rocked the boat. Instead of the usual bass-like sequence of runs and rests, the pull on my line was hard and unrelenting, like hauling in an old tire or rubber boot. After an arduous, half-hour fight, I hefted a three-foot American eel into our rowboat—jaws snapping and thick body thrashing about.

We continued fishing for another two hours or so. When our prow finally returned to shore, I waded into the shallows to clean off the eel and noticed that its gills were moving. "It's still alive!" I yelled. Believing it deserved to go free after surviving such an ordeal, I released it in the shallow waters and watched it swim lazily away.

Many years later, after moving to Vermont, I learned that the American eel (*Anguilla rostrata*) was once an important food source for the Abenaki peoples of northern New England. Autumn eels were captured in stone weirs as they migrated downstream. Traps consisted of two short lines of rocks that met in the shape of a V pointing downriver. An eel pot—a round basket with a wide mouth—was placed where the rocks converged.

The catch consisted mostly of reproductively mature female American eels (called *silver eels*) that were swimming to midwinter spawning grounds in the Sargasso Sea, south of Bermuda. Each female produces 15 to 20 million eggs that hatch into larvae. The larvae drift northward on ocean currents, transforming into minute, clear *glass eels*. Eventually the young eels become greenish-brown *elvers*, when they begin their springtime journey up estuaries and rivers.

Young eels are only about an inch long when they reach the coast. Males often remain in brackish waters while the diminutive females swim slowly upstream until they enter the deep waters of lakes. There they develop into *yellow eels* and live for some 6 to 30 years, feeding mostly at night on small fish, frogs, crustaceans, insects, worms, and shellfish. Females, which are larger than males, can grow to over 3 feet long. Sexually mature silver eels begin a nocturnal journey downstream during the autumn. After entering the ocean, they stop eating and swim back to the Sargasso Sea—there to spawn—and die.

Eels can still be found in my old stomping grounds of southern New England, as well as in certain places in southern New Hampshire and Vermont. In northern New England, however, eels have experienced a rapid decline and become scarce. Some populations have disappeared altogether. From Lake Champlain to the Chesapeake Bay, and from Lake Ontario to the Connecticut River, eel populations are falling.

Why the decline? "Eels were shut off from their historic growing areas beginning with the first dams across the Connecticut River in the 1790s," says David Deen, river steward for the Connecticut River Watershed Council. Young eels can't leap obstacles the way salmon and shad can. "They make their way by pushing against the rough surface of rocks where there is a light flow of water. Eel ladders are like indoor-outdoor carpeting with a trickle flow of

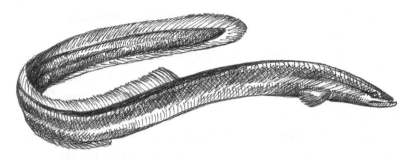

water." A number of hydropower dams have installed eel ladders, and existing fish ladders are gradually being modified to accommodate eels.

At one hydroelectric dam on the upper St. Lawrence River, the number of eels passing dropped from 27,500 per day in 1982 to 50 per day in 2004. In 2002, a mere 275 American eels passed the Holyoke Dam in Massachusetts; by 2005 the number of eels passing the dam generally ranged from few to none. Although some local and regional eel populations (like ours in the Northeast) have declined, the U.S. Fish and Wildlife Service has concluded that the overall population is not endangered and does not warrant protection under the Endangered Species Act.

Hydroelectric dams are particularly harmful to seagoing females. Between 80 and 100 percent can be injured passing through hydro-turbine blades, with up to half being killed. Many eels must traverse several dams while migrating downstream. Some hydropower companies now shut turbines off at night during peak autumn eel migration. Several defunct dams have been removed, restoring eel habitat and improving water quality.

Overharvesting may also be playing a role. The use of eels for food is increasing worldwide, especially in Europe and Asia where glass eels are a delicacy; the price in 2014 ranged from $600 to $800 per pound. In the Northeast, two states—Maine and New York—permit the commercial harvest of silver eels. Because eels spawn only once in a lifetime, adults that are caught have never reproduced.

Habitat loss and water pollution also adversely affect eels. Toxins that accumulate in eel fat can reduce growth, decrease reproduction, threaten the survival of young, and lower resistance to diseases and parasites. Pollution can disorient eels and reduce both their ability to mate and their endurance for swimming. The concentrations of mercury, PCBs, and other contaminants in eels from Lake Champlain are so high that women of childbearing age and children under fifteen are advised to abstain from eating them.

Like many aquatic animals, eels also face threats posed by climate change. Eventually, warming at the ocean's surface may shift the flow of the Gulf Stream and other major ocean currents that carry young eels northward from the spawning grounds.

Perhaps, with concerted effort, American eels will one day be restored to their historic range in New England. Biologists are constructing eelways for elver passage around dams, as well as working to remove disused dams, which reestablishes eel habitat and improves water quality.

At the local level, many sewage treatment plants and drainage systems are being upgraded to prevent stormwater runoff from mixing with sewage and entering waterways during heavy rains. In some towns, highway crews have begun to install culverts that are submerged at both ends, and large enough so that eels, and other fish and aquatic organisms can pass through.

What can individuals do to assist the American eel recovery? In addition to doing our part to reduce global climate change, the best way for individuals to help is to support groups that are working on long-term actions, such as the Connecticut River Watershed Council. Contact your power company and encourage them to allow water to flow over hydroelectric dams during the eel's autumn migration downstream. Encourage them to build special eelways alongside fish ladders, and to dismantle idle dams.

If you do catch an eel and decide to eat it, look for a rice-sized glass chip with tiny wires inside. These magnetic tags are implanted by biologists who monitor eel movements. In July 2004, ten-year-old Dakota Folmsbee caught a 39-inch American eel in southern Lake Champlain that contained one of these tags. His father gave the tag to a biologist from the Vermont Fish and Wildlife Department, who eventually determined that the eel had been caught and tagged seven years earlier at the Chambly Eel Ladder along the Richelieu River, 100 miles to the north.

Re-establishing the eel would enable native peoples to practice a venerable tradition. In the 1980s, members of the Abenaki Nation of Vermont hoped to start a limited eel fishery in Lake Champlain, but scarce eels and poor market conditions made the venture unsustainable. Eels clearly remind us that our own well-being is closely intertwined with the fate of the natural world.

# Minute Mussel
# Makes Big Splash

WHEN ANDY WARHOL SAID everyone would have fifteen minutes of fame, he wasn't talking about invertebrates. But in March 1987 the dwarf wedge mussel garnered national attention when Plainfield, New Hampshire, adopted it as the "town mollusk." Plainfield's stretch of the Connecticut River harbors one of the last remaining populations of this rare bivalve.

The diminutive mussel may not be as spectacular as other endangered species, such as the Canada lynx or the timber rattlesnake, but it endeared itself to Plainfield's residents. Nancy Mogielnicki, a physician's assistant and one of the community's chief mussel advocates, jokingly suggested, some thirty years ago, that the town designate its critical habitat as "Mussel Beach." Mogielnicki now reports that all is quiet on the mussel front: No recent publicity efforts have been launched as the mussels continue their filter-feeding ways. Yet their future remains uncertain.

The dwarf wedge mussel, *Alasmidonta heterodon*, was first discovered at nearby Sumner's Falls during the 1800s. This series of falls lies between Plainfield and Hartland, Vermont, about halfway between the Connecticut River's source and Long Island Sound. It is among the last free-flowing stretches remaining along the river's 400-mile course.

Viable populations of the mussel are now found in only about twenty places on the Atlantic Coast. These include locations on the Ashuelot and Connecticut Rivers in New Hampshire and Vermont, as well as stretches of rivers in Maryland, Connecticut, Massachusetts, New York, New Jersey, Pennsylvania, Virginia, and North Carolina. The mussel is listed as endan-

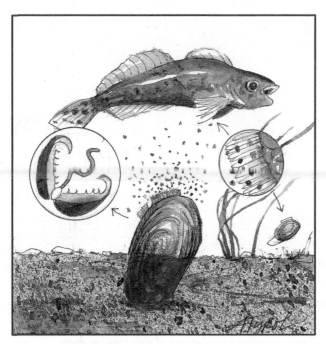

*Life cycle of dwarf wedge mussel.*

gered by the states of Vermont and New Hampshire and by the federal government.

The mussel, which lives in roiling water below rapids and waterfalls, is threatened by changes to its habitat. The species needs clean, swift-moving, well-oxygenated water. Its populations began ebbing in the late eighteenth century, when dams were constructed along many of the region's rivers, eliminating the free-flowing waters needed to maintain the mussel's habitat.

Mussels have difficulty adapting to the changes in water level and temperature caused by fluctuations in flows, both above and below dams. Mussels can't survive in the deep, slow-moving water upstream from dams because it is warmer, has lower oxygen levels, and tends to be more acid. In this altered environment the river's current slows, allowing sediments to more readily settle to the bottom, clogging the mussels' gills and covering what might otherwise be the kind of well-oxygenated beds of sand, silt, and gravel where the mussels thrive. Riverbank erosion, caused by vacillating water levels and waves from boat traffic, only exacerbates the sedimentation problem.

The mussel is also threatened by pollution in the form of toxic chemicals and nutrient runoff, and by the decline of some populations of fish species that serve as hosts for their larvae.

Beds of the nearly two-inch-long, greenish-brown, iridescent mussels anchor themselves in the bottom sediments where they filter tiny plants, animals, and bits of debris from the water for food. In mid to late July, the males shed sperm into the water, where females can use it to fertilize the eggs, which they shelter in their gills. Fertilized eggs develop into larvae, called veligers, that overwinter in the gills.

When veligers are released in April or May, they spend their first days attached to the fins of a fish, but they're so small that the fish are unharmed. Only a few larvae are able to find a suitable host fish on which to attach and metamorphose into an adult; the rest don't survive. According to Michael Marchand—a wildlife biologist for New Hampshire's Nongame and Endangered Species Program—possible host fish include Atlantic salmon and two small bottom-feeders: the slimy sculpin and the tessellated darter, which is especially common in the mussel's Connecticut River habitat. Soon, the larvae grow into small versions of the adult form and drop off to live on the river bottom. Since the adults move about very little, the juvenile period of hitchhiking on fish is important for helping mussels disperse.

Despite its complex life cycle and narrow habitat requirements, the mussel still lives in the rapids that stretch between Plainfield and Hartland, because the river's flow at Sumner's Falls has remained relatively unaltered. It is also found in the Connecticut River between Charlestown, New Hampshire, and Springfield, Vermont, and between Lancaster, New Hampshire, and Lunenberg, Vermont. In addition, it has been found in scattered locations from Haverhill and Newbury to Orford and Fairlee, according to the U.S. Fish and Wildlife Service.

The dwarf wedge mussel may keep a low profile, but their populations are of interest to aquatic biologists—who consider it the underwater version of the canary in the coal mine. Because the mollusk is so sensitive to environmental changes, a drop in their population may signal possible changes in water quality. It also can serve as a biological barometer for helping to safeguard other mussel species in the Connecticut, among them the brook floater mussel, a close relative.

The dwarf wedge mussel's fate mirrors that of freshwater mussels found throughout North America, where twenty species have been extirpated and roughly a hundred are endangered. In fact, nearly half of the continent's species of freshwater mussels have now become extinct or are on the brink, making this one of our most rapidly disappearing groups of animals.

While the dwarf wedge mussel's celebrity has waned, not every endangered species is fortunate enough to reside in Plainfield—a community that likes to flex its environmental muscle and just happens to think that its tiny Town Mollusk is kind of cute.

# Spring Peepers, Winter Sleepers

IN THE REALM OF NATURE, mysteries often unfold beyond the limits of our perception. Not so with spring peepers. Stand at the edge of any wetland when peepers have reached full voice, and you will be engulfed in the world of another species. A piercing chorus of hundreds of males will wash over your sensory shores. The mating calls of the spring peeper are nature's choir fortissimo—pulsing, sonic sleigh bells.

Peepers awake from their winter slumber, sometimes with snow still on the ground, ready to reproduce. During the previous autumn, the bodies of these tiny chorus frogs began their physiological preparations for the next mating season, a strategy that allows them to start the spring cycle as early as possible. Some males become so well prepared that they begin calling before winter arrives. In my nature journal, I have recorded hearing these "fall peepers" well into foliage season and beyond: one peeper began singing on December 7, 1998, as the temperature reached the mid-50s.

When autumn wanes and temperatures drop below freezing, how does a one-inch frog survive the winter if all it does is snuggle beneath leaf litter or under a log or tree root? As a peeper's temperature gradually drops, sugars begin to concentrate inside its cells and compose a kind of natural antifreeze. Individual cells expel much of their water so that ice, when it begins to form in small amounts, is confined to the spaces between cells, where its sharp edges won't damage the cell contents or a peeper's internal organs. Still, this strategy only works so well; a dormant peeper will freeze and die at temperatures below about 21 degrees Fahrenheit, so insulating snow cover (and a nice blanket of leaves and duff) is crucial. Wood frogs and gray tree frogs employ a similar winter survival strategy.

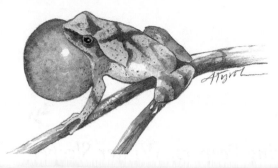

Even though a spring peeper in winter is dormant and its body is cold, its cells and organs still need some energy to stay alive. But its body is receiving neither the oxygen nor the nutrients that would normally circulate in the blood of an active animal. To get around this, the peeper relies on energy stored the previous autumn. The same sugar that acts as antifreeze in the dormant peeper's cells also serves as a source of nourishment, as do glycogen reserves stored in its organs. These carbohydrates slowly ferment to provide a bit of energy for the sluggish metabolism of the dormant "peepsicle."

As these carbohydrate supplies dwindle in early spring, peepers wake up and migrate to marshes, bushy swamps, woodland pools, and the edges of ponds. This is the easiest time to find the tiny frogs, whose skin can vary from tan to brown, gray, or olive-green. Look for the dark brown, X-shaped cross that marks their backs, which gives rise to the species name of *crucifer*. The ¾-inch males are smaller than the females, which can grow to be 1¼ inches long.

Males start to call as early as mid-March in southern New England. They inflate a dark, olive-colored throat pouch to nearly the size of their body and use it to push air over their vocal cords, repeating this cycle to make a sound both when they inhale and exhale. Each piercing call rises in a crescendo. Listen closely to a peeper chorus and you'll soon realize that they play off each other, engaging in duets, trios, quartets, and more. Sometimes you can hear the bird-like trill that males use to defend modest mating territories, which range from about 4 to 16 inches across.

Peepers have an uncanny knack for positioning themselves so that the surrounding leaves and stems amplify their calls and cause them to sound as if they are emanating from somewhere else—a kind of natural ventriloquism. Combine this with the ability to change their skin color to match the environment, and with sticky toe pads that can cling to virtually any surface, and it's not surprising that patience—and often a strong flashlight—are required to actually see a peeper calling.

When a female approaches a singing male and touches him to indicate her amorous intent, he climbs onto her back and holds on tight as she swims around the marsh or pond. Males fertilize up to 800 eggs as they emerge from the female, who deposits the eggs individually or in small clusters on submerged vegetation. Females then retreat from the pond while their diminutive Don Juans continue to serenade for weeks, a few even crooning until the fireflies begin to sparkle.

Peeper populations are healthy throughout New England. They thrive in wetlands and will reproduce as long as long as the water is not too acidic, requiring a pH above 4. Fortunately, spring peepers aren't experiencing the widespread growth deformities, such as missing limbs and digits, affecting some other local species of frogs. At the moment, the state of these boisterous and endearing little creatures is as bright as their familiar ringing calls.

# INTERRELATIONSHIPS

# Saplappers and Bugnappers

## THE KEYSTONE SAPSUCKERS

WHILE OUT FOR A WALK one midsummer day, I heard a loud buzz and looked up to marvel at a hummingbird moving methodically along the bark of a basswood tree, lapping up the sap that oozed from small holes chiseled by a yellow-bellied sapsucker. Although the sapsucker is saddled with a name that sounds like an insult, it plays a critical role in the lives of hummingbirds and many other animals.

Yellow-bellied sapsuckers are lively birds with sporty plumage. Pastel yellow feathers on the breast are highlighted by a bright red cap and striking zigzag bars of black and white on each side of the head and neck. They also have a white wing stripe and a red neck with a bib-like black crescent.

The name "sapsucker" comes from their habit of pecking neat, horizontal rows of holes in tree bark. Male sapsuckers migrate northward earlier than females, in late March or early April, in order to establish breeding territories. As soon as the sapsuckers return, they start pecking lattice-like patterns of ¼-inch holes across trunks and branches to tap into the sap of the inner bark (phloem) that carries sugar and other nutrients down from the treetops. Maple-syrup makers drill deeper holes to tap the sapwood (xylem). That sap contains from 2 to 3 percent sugar, while the phloem sap consumed by sapsuckers may contain 20 to 30 percent sugar.

Sapsuckers use brush-like tongues to lap the sap that accumulates at the top of each hole. They periodically clean out and renew the holes to keep the sap flowing. Once the flow subsides, sapsuckers move up the bark and start another row of holes. They're especially fond of tapping basswood, apple,

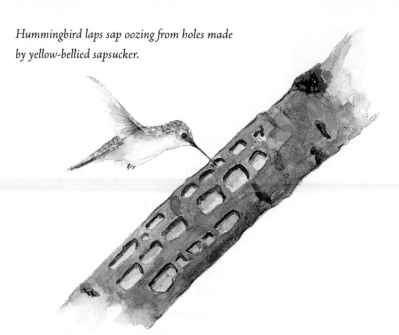

*Hummingbird laps sap oozing from holes made by yellow-bellied sapsucker.*

hemlock, sugar maple, aspen, white birch, and mountain ash. They also eat cambium and inner bark as they chisel, along with a smorgasbord of insects, especially ants, which can comprise up to a third of their diet.

The mix of sugar and other nutrients contained in the sweet sap is similar to flower nectar, so it's no surprise that the northernmost range of the ruby-throated hummingbird coincides with the summer breeding territory of the yellow-bellied sapsucker. When hummingbirds arrive in New England in early spring, there are enough sapsucker holes already exuding sweet sap to supplement the nectar from early-blooming flowers. Hummingbirds continue to feed on sapsucker holes throughout the summer—they even shadow sapsuckers making the rounds of the best sap wells, chasing away other birds (except for sapsuckers) that come to feed.

But the impact of sapsucker activity extends well beyond hummingbirds. Their sap wells are nature's soda fountains for about three dozen different species of birds, including other woodpeckers, yellow-rumped warblers, Cape May warblers, eastern phoebes, ruby-crowned kinglets, nuthatches, and chickadees. The sap also nourishes a host of mammals, including squirrels, bats, and porcupines, along with insects from at least twenty different families, such as bees, wasps, hornets and moths.

Some animals, like red squirrels, feed directly on the sap, while many others, including hummingbirds, also feast on insects drawn to the sweetness. Some fungi colonize the oozing sap, including one called "black bark" that forms dark, canker-like patches. Many bacteria and fungi that can decay and discolor wood enter trees through sapsucker holes.

*Yellow-bellied sapsucker.*

Studies show that species diversity, as well as population size within each species, are greater in forests with high levels of sapsucker activity. Because of this effect, sapsuckers are considered a *keystone species*—they have a critical impact on the surrounding ecological community that goes beyond what would normally be expected from their numbers.

Beavers are another example of a keystone species—their ponds provide critical food, water, and cover for an array of plants and animals. Late sleepers, however, might describe sapsuckers as more of a hammer-stone species, as males bang their notoriously loud "rat-a-tat-tat" territorial calls on metal roofs, chimney caps, and other resonant surfaces.

In our region, sapsuckers often chisel nest holes in the punky wood of aging aspens infected with white trunk rot fungus. They also nest in cottonwood, beech, pine, fir, maple, birch, elm, butternut, willow, and alder. Females lay from two to seven white eggs; these are incubated by both sexes. Hatchlings call incessantly for adults to bring insect meals, some of which are coated in sweet sap—like a bug fondue.

Sapsuckers lap at their sap wells several times a day throughout the growing season. As summer advances and the sap of some species wanes, sapsuckers tap other species of trees, searching for the best sap flow at any particular time. They also supplement their diet with more insects and partake of ripening berries and nuts. Overall, their signature sap-tapping has a positive influence on the world around them, even as it remains the source of their dubious moniker.

# Pine on the Cob

A FEW SUMMERS AGO, I saw a red squirrel skittering along the top of a stone wall with something in its mouth. I snuck in closer and discovered the headless body of a chipmunk dangling from its jaws. Prior to that, I'd viewed red squirrels as curmudgeonly little herbivores, not wolves in squirrel's clothing. It was as if Bugs Bunny had eaten the head off of Alvin the chipmunk.

The cantankerous red squirrels are opportunistic feeders. Their diet consists mostly of vegetarian fare, but in addition to eating nuts, bark, roots, fruit, fungi, buds, and flowers, they'll partake of everything from insects, eggs, and baby birds to small reptiles, amphibians, mice, baby rabbits, and even cast-off antlers.

During the winter, red squirrels subsist on seeds of conifers and may eat up to two-thirds of the seed crop produced in a forest each year. Staples include the seeds of spruce, eastern hemlock, pine, cedar, and larch. They also eat the seeds of many hardwoods, such as basswood, box elder, sycamore, red oak, hickory, and maple. One study of captive red squirrels found that each squirrel consumed the seeds from an average of 144 white spruce cones

each day. Because Norway spruce cones contain numerous high-energy seeds that store especially well, groves of this tree can harbor four to five times the number of red squirrels found in other conifer forests.

I've observed red squirrels biting off white pine cones, which landed with a "thump" about every ten seconds. While watching a squirrel forage amid Norway spruce, I saw it carry away cones almost as long as its 7-inch body. Most cones are cached in the shade of mature conifers—hoarded for the winter, either individually or in mounds called middens that are secreted underground, beneath rocks, or in a hollow tree. A red squirrel's acute sense of smell can detect seed caches buried under a foot of soil and beneath snow up to 12 feet deep. Yet food is not retrieved from every larder, so squirrels inadvertently plant seeds in forgotten caches and spread the spores of beneficial fungi.

In a fascinating study of red squirrel behavior conducted in a grove of Norway spruce in Norwich, Vermont, ecologist Fritz Gerhardt found that they habitually raid each other's middens. On average, each squirrel lost about a quarter of its seeds to its neighbors, while simultaneously stealing about the same proportion of seeds from surrounding middens. However, some squirrels pilfered far more seeds than they lost, and vice versa, so the actual balance varied between neighboring squirrels.

A red squirrel will frequent the base of a particular pine tree to eat, chewing scales off the cone in the same way that people eat corn on the cob. First, it chews the scales off near the stem. As each scale falls away, a pair of seeds is exposed. Because each subsequent scale lies up the cone and a small turn along the spiral, the squirrel must twirl the cone as it eats. Mounds of discarded scales and naked cone-cores pile up wherever a red squirrel partakes of its pine-on-the-cob.

Terminal conifer buds are another winter staple. Red squirrels harvest buds like they do cones, using the gnaw-and-drop method. They also munch the buds of maples and birches. In some spruce forests, I've seen the ground littered with thousands of branch tips. Although red squirrels look comically mischievous with their black eyes surrounded by white rings, their heavy harvest of seeds and buds, and their penchant for eating the bark of young trees, can seriously damage conifers and their ability to regenerate.

But red squirrels don't just gnaw the winter away. When not active by day, they hunker down in tree hollows, rocky enclaves, and underground burrows. During extreme cold, these solitary creatures sometimes share shelters. Otherwise they defend territories with vociferous screeches, buzzes, and grating, rhythmic chortlings. In good coniferous forest, red squirrel territories can be as large as 2 acres.

They breed from about mid-January through mid-February, often during thaws. Dens are in hollow trees, especially old woodpecker nests. Litters of two to five hairless squirrel-lets arrive about a month after mating. Young grow quickly under the female's care, start to wander from the nest at around six weeks, and are weaned in about two months. Goshawks, martens, red-tailed hawks, ermines, red foxes, and other predators eat so many young that only a quarter survive to reproduce the following year.

As winter progresses and sap starts to flow, red squirrels sometimes chew holes in the bark of sugar maples and other hardwoods. After the sap oozes out and evaporation concentrates the sugar, the squirrels return to lap up the sweetness. The Europeans who first came to New England learned maple sugaring from indigenous peoples, but we'll never know how red squirrels figured it out. That closely guarded secret is only handed down on a need to gnaw basis.

# Nature's Own Herbicides

ANYONE WHO GREW UP in a large family knows how much time is expended competing for food, space, and attention. Who is going to be served dinner first, get the best seat at the movies, or enjoy the last dollop of ice cream? At times, the jousting can become serious and, well, impolite. Someone always gets short shrift, and it's no different in the natural world.

Plants also compete: they vie for air, water, space, sunshine, and nutrients. And while they can't protest or push to be first in line, plants do deploy chemicals to obtain an advantage over other species. This process is called *allelopathy*, which comes from the Greek words *pathos*, "to suffer," and *allelon*, "of each other." This phenomenon was first recorded in 300 B.C., when it was observed that barley, chickpeas, and other cultivated plants interfered with the growth of other crops. Allelopathy is responsible for the killed grass beneath bird feeders where the hulls of sunflower seeds have fallen. And it is why gardeners plant wormwood away from the herbs whose growth it inhibits, such as sage, anise, fennel, and caraway.

Many native plants compete with other species using allelochemicals. Black walnut and butternut contain juglone, which is concentrated in the nut husks, roots, and buds. This compound inhibits the growth of many plants, including apples, blueberries, and azaleas, and especially those in the nightshade family, such as peppers, tomatoes, and potatoes. Since a black walnut's root system can reach well beyond the edge of the crown's expanse, the ground is often bare far from the trunk. Hickories, pecan, and English walnut also produce juglone, but in smaller concentrations.

Allelochemicals act in myriad ways. Compounds that inhibit plant growth and seed germination are emitted from roots and can leach out of leaves,

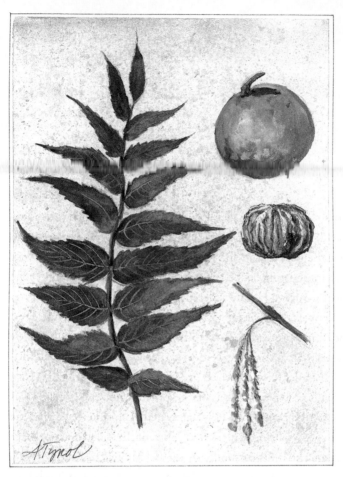

*Black walnut* (CLOCKWISE FROM LEFT): *compound leaf, fruit (with husk), nut, flower.*

twigs, flowers, and seed casings. Some plants exude chemicals that suppress the activity of chlorophyll in the leaves of other species, diminishing their ability to use sunlight to create carbohydrates for growth. Other allelochemicals impede the ability of roots to absorb water and nutrients. The leaves of some species give off toxic gases.

Hay-scented fern is an indigenous plant that many foresters and ecologists long suspected of being allelopathic, because it forms broad swaths through which tree seedlings struggle to grow, especially those of black cherry and sugar maple. Studies conducted by the University of Vermont's Proctor Maple

Research Center, however, show that this fern is simply a strong competitor. Its dense crowns block sunlight, and the thick mats of roots out-compete tree seedlings for water and nutrients. White pine and black birch seedlings fare better in hay-scented fern beds because their spring leaves open before the fronds of fern unfurl.

Plants have probably used allelopathy to compete with each other since the early stages of evolution. Over time, the dynamic between indigenous species reaches a sort of balance, with any particular outcome depending on a variety of factors, including the type of soil, the amount of rainfall, and the pressure of browsing animals. Among other native plants that are suspected of using some form of allelopathy are sugar maple, American elm, red oak, sunflower, cottonwood, American sycamore, black cherry, sassafras, and tobacco. In fact, extracts from the wood of red maple and eastern red-cedar inhibit seed germination at least as strongly as do extracts from black walnut.

Some plants that have been introduced to New England from other environments—so-called "alien species"—are also allelopathic. Japanese knotweed is infamous for its ability to stifle other plant species. The roots of this invasive plant produce substances that are growth-inhibiting and poisonous to other plants. Japanese knotweed also creates a dense cover of leaves that virtually prevents sunshine from reaching the ground.

Garlic mustard, another alien species, creates a compound that harms the intricate relationship between the roots of certain native trees and the mycorrhizal fungi with which they associate in the soil. In this symbiotic relationship, found among birches, beeches, maples, some conifers, and possibly other trees, the plant roots that are penetrated by fungal threads pass water and carbohydrates to the fungi. In turn, the fungal threads expand the root's ability to absorb nutrients from the soil. Garlic mustard interrupts this mutually beneficial connection.

Whether a plant is a native species or introduced from afar, allelopathic competition plays a part in its ecological role. From forests and wetlands to gardens and fields, allelochemicals contribute to the dynamic of plant interactions. Nature's deceptively serene appearance belies the struggles being waged unseen. It's not hard for us to relate; simply picture the intense sibling rivalries that create shifting lines of competition during family visits, especially those of the holiday season.

# Of Cuckoos and Caterpillars

THE CATERPILLARS OF 2006 brought the summer of our discontent. They seemed to be everywhere, eating the leaves off ornamental apple and cherry trees, defoliating black cherry trees in fence lines, and even munching their way across whole hillsides of sugar maples. But our nightmare of writhing critters was the stuff of dreams for black-billed cuckoos, which had been arriving in large numbers that summer to feast on their favorite foodstuff, the tent caterpillar. The call of the black-billed cuckoo was often heard amid the chorus of our common summer birds.

Our local relative of the European species of cuckoo-clock fame, and of the roadrunner that lives in the desert Southwest, is often heard but rarely seen. The black-billed cuckoo is nearly a foot long with brownish, olive-colored feathers tinged with bronze along the top of its head and back. It is off-white underneath, from the black beak down to the tail. Look through binoculars to see the reddish eye-ring and the faint white stripes across the undersides of the tail feathers, which are also tipped with white. Cuckoos are graceful flyers, but their down-curved beak and posture cause them to appear slightly humped when perched.

The song ("coo-coo-coo, coo-coo-coo, coo-coo-coo") reminds me of the lugubrious notes of the mourning dove, only sung in quick, succeeding triplets and with a hard "c" in front of each note.

Cuckoos possess a ready appetite for caterpillars and they appear in great numbers during years when there is an outbreak of the bristle-coated buggers—those ravenous eastern tent caterpillars of early summer, the forest tent caterpillars of midsummer, or the fall webworms of late summer.

The bodies of these larvae are the lepidopteran versions of a fuzzy peach, and most birds prefer their larvae hairless, thank you. The stiff hairs build up and cause discomfort in the stomach linings of many birds that eat them. Birds that are known to feed on the occasional pubescent caterpillar include the eastern towhee, brown thrasher, gray catbird, rose-breasted grosbeak, scarlet tanager, American crow, and ring-necked pheasant. Ground-feeding American robins and common flickers may also partake. Northern orioles sometimes eat the soft innards and leave the hairy skins behind.

*Black-billed cuckoo.*

But cuckoos are true dietary specialists, adapted to eating the hirsute larvae whose multitudes periodically overrun our parks and woodlands. Over time, a cuckoo's stomach becomes felted with caterpillar hairs that stick in the lining. Eventually this felt becomes so dense that it inhibits digestion, so the cuckoo sheds its whole stomach lining and grows a new one.

During a caterpillar population boom, like the one in 2006, caterpillars can account for two-thirds of a cuckoo's diet. Some studies have found more than 100 caterpillars at a time in cuckoos' stomachs, with one black-billed cuckoo weighing in with 250 young tent caterpillars in its gut. Another individual was seen devouring three dozen caterpillars in five minutes. Cuckoos will also eat berries, beetles, crickets, grasshoppers, cicadas, katydids, aquatic insects, small fish, and even the eggs and young of other birds.

The periods when caterpillars are abundant are ideal for seeking out the nests of these retiring birds. If you see a cuckoo, watch it and try to discover where it is flying to tend its young, a task shared by both sexes. I once discovered an active black-billed cuckoo nest snuggled close to the main trunk of a Norway spruce, about 15 feet off the ground.

Nests are usually built in a dense shrub or where a branch grows horizontally from a tree trunk, from 2 to 20 feet up. A base of twigs is woven and lined with dry leaves, pine needles, catkins, and the cottony puffs of seeds. Eggs are a solid, dull greenish-blue and a bit more than an inch long. Two to four eggs are laid in the nest, and they hatch in about two weeks. More eggs are laid during years when caterpillars are abundant, helping the cuckoo population increase during caterpillar outbreaks. Eggs of black-billed cuckoos have also been discovered in the nests of other birds, including those of the cardinal, chipping sparrow, wood thrush, cedar waxwing, eastern wood-pewee, yellow warbler, gray catbird, and even the yellow-billed cuckoo.

If you get too close to a cuckoo nest, you may provoke a territorial display during which the tail is fanned and wings are spread wide, evoking a feathered cape. Fledgling chicks have been known to go limp and play dead if threatened.

The next time you are out on a cuculiform ("cuckoo-related") quest, be sure to don a cucullate ("hood-like") cap, or the constant rain of caterpillar castings might cause you to cuss. And if the cuckoos are vocalizing more than usual, you may want to bring a raincoat as well: the calls of these "rain crows" are rumored to be most frequent just before a storm.

And don't let the sunset stifle your quest: cuckoos frequently sing on languid summer nights. It is a rare joy to watch fireflies flash while being serenaded by a cuckoo. Look for a fleeting silhouette against the lunar orb.

# Big, Bold, and Rusty

## INVASIVE CRAYFISH HAS CLAWS

INVASIVE SPECIES don't always arrive in North America from a distant shore: in the bilge of a boat from Asia, for example, or in a shipment of wood from Europe. Some species, like the rusty crayfish, come from other states.

Normally, crayfish don't move very far; certain species are only found in a single watershed. So how did the rusty crayfish travel from its native range in the Ohio River Valley to New England?

"Primarily, they're used as baitfish and then released into waterways," says Leslie Matthews, an environmental scientist with the Vermont Department of Environmental Conservation's Watershed Management Division. "They're also sold as aquarium species, then dumped when people empty their aquaria into waterways. Some get released after being used for classroom study. Commercial harvesters also move rusties around."

The rusty crayfish, *Orconectes rusticus*, has hitchhiked as far as Ontario, New Mexico, and Maryland, and is now found in more than a dozen states, including New York and every New England state but Rhode Island. Having first been recorded in Vermont in the 1970s, Matthews says that it is now "widely distributed in the Connecticut River and its tributaries and is dominant in the White River." It is also found in Lake Morey in Fairlee and in Lake Carmi in northwestern Vermont.

"Only three species of crayfish are native to Vermont," says Matthews, "but another five species have been introduced. In 2010, for the first time, the big water crayfish (*Cambarus robustus*) showed up in the White River. This crayfish species appears to have been introduced recently, which suggests that people are still moving crayfish around and releasing them in the water. Therefore, the threat of the spread of rusty crayfish, as well as potential for other invasive introductions, continues to be high."

Once a plant or animal is removed from its indigenous habitat and dropped into a new environment, it escapes the normal checks that keep it in balance with its surroundings, such as predation and competition. Most such species don't survive in the new location, but those that do can create an ensuing "invasion" whose effects range from a slightly skewed food chain to the complete elimination of some native species.

At first glance, a rusty crayfish doesn't look like an impending ecological disaster. Up to 4 inches long, it is somewhat bigger than our native species. The adult's reddish-brown shell, or carapace, has a rust-colored spot on each side which, says Matthews, "looks like someone with red paint on their thumb and forefinger picked one up by the sides, like a lobster." The black tip on each

TOP  *Rusty crayfish.*
BOTTOM  *Female rusty crayfish and eggs.*

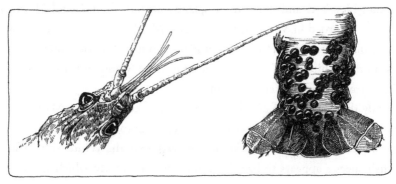

claw is another giveaway. These markings are easier to see when the animal is underwater.

Character and habit, as well as size, have earned this rapacious crustacean its notoriety. Rusty crayfish are aggressive and can eat four times the volume consumed by native species, out-competing local crayfish for homes and food. Their diet includes the bottom-dwelling insects and mollusks that are essential sources of energy for the aquatic food chain—from mayflies and stoneflies to leeches, snails, and water fleas.

Rusties will even eat the eggs and young of native fish, including those of the bluegill and pumpkinseed. They can denude a river bottom of plants, destroying habitat and nursery grounds for fish and other animals. Their swift movements elude predaceous fish better than native species and churn up silt from the bottom.

If this weren't enough, rusty crayfish hybridize with our native northern clearwater crayfish (*Orconectes propinquus*). One study in a Wisconsin lake found that, through competition and interbreeding, rusty crayfish supplanted and genetically assimilated the lake's entire population of clearwater crayfish. Eventually, all of the crayfish looked just like rusties and only one-quarter of the population had any northern clearwater crayfish genes remaining.

Rusties mate in the autumn; females then store the sperm until the following spring, when they can lay 500 or more eggs. As a result, transporting a single fertile female into a new environment can easily start a new population. And once the rusty crayfish becomes established, no form of management or control seems to keep it in check. Intensive trapping decreases numbers, but it has not been shown to eliminate the population.

It's critical to know how to identify rusty crayfish and prevent them from spreading. Boaters must be sure that no crayfish or other invasive species are attached to a boat, motor, or trailer, and bilge water should be drained at the boat ramp before leaving a lake, river, or pond. Rather than releasing unused baitfish into the environment, anglers should freeze them and then compost the remains.

"If you trap crayfish," says Matthews, "only use them where caught. Don't dump your aquarium, and don't buy crayfish from out of state, including the Internet. It's now illegal to import crayfish species into Vermont without a permit."

PATTERNS &
PERCEPTIONS

# April Fools

## NATURE'S MYTHS AND MISBELIEFS

WALKING THROUGH THE WOODS on a cool spring morning, I saw a barred owl in an old maple tree. I circled the owl three times from a distance. Its head kept turning to follow me, tracking my movements with three complete revolutions.

One of the owl's chicks had fallen from the nest, so I climbed the tree and placed the chick back in it. Then the owl flew up and pushed the chick out of the nest and onto the ground, where it lay in a pile of melting snow.

I noticed that the maple was the biggest tree in sight, so it had to be the oldest. A rusty sap bucket hung from the tree on a tap that had probably been forgotten some fifteen years ago. The bucket, which had originally been placed four feet off the ground, was now ten feet high, having moved up as the tree grew.

On the way home, I passed a fallen tree and contemplated how it must have landed silently because no one had been there to hear it.

A cute baby skunk was hiding in a hollow under the tree. I stuck my head in to have a good look, because I knew that immature skunks couldn't spray. Then I saw a porcupine, but when I bent down to see it close-up, it shot several quills into my neck.

Running home in excruciating pain, I heard a bear off in the distance. It had just emerged from hibernation and was hooting to find a mate.

When I got home I rushed through the door and into the mudroom. I looked at the calendar and noticed the date: April 1. Then I heard the alarm go off, and I woke up.

THIS IMAGINARY DREAM was spun from misbeliefs that have survived generations of retelling, with surprising tenacity. Here are descriptions of eight common myths, followed by the corresponding truths. (Many thanks to the staff of the Springfield office of Vermont's Agency of Natural Resources for sharing their favorite nature misconceptions.)

*An owl can turn its head 360 degrees.* While it looks like an owl can spin its head completely around, the head actually moves a maximum of 270 degrees in either direction. Say you're looking at an owl that has already turned its head as far as it can go to the right; it then turns its head back to the forward position and keeps turning as far as it can to the left. In this case, its head will have rotated leftward by a total of 540 degrees—1½ complete revolutions. The structure of an owl's neck vertebrae, along with specially adapted blood vessels, enable these extreme motions. (Red-tailed hawks can turn their heads nearly as far as owls.)

*Barred owl.*

*If you touch a baby bird that has fallen from its nest, then put it back, the parents will reject it.* Adults will not abandon a chick just because a person touched it. If you find a baby chick on the ground, search overhead for the nest and gently place the chick back in it. Many "baby birds" found on the ground are really fledglings who are learning to fly. If a juvenile bird has young feathers, is awkwardly flying near the ground, and can perch on your finger, then place it on a nearby branch and the parents will find it.

*The biggest trees are the oldest trees.* Growth rate depends on a combination of genes and growing conditions. Some species (white pine, cottonwood) grow quickly, while others (white oak, hickory) grow more slowly. A 50-year-old red oak that is growing in fertile soil with plenty of sunlight might be 16 inches in diameter, while a red oak of similar age that is competing with other trees in poor growing conditions might only be 10 inches across. A shagbark hickory of the same size, growing nearby, could be 75 years old.

*A nail driven into a tree moves up as the tree grows.* Trees only grow upward from the tips of the branches. A nail or sugaring tap driven or drilled into the side of a tree will remain at the same height over time. The bole, or trunk, of a tree grows outward, so eventually the nail or hole will be engulfed by wood.

*Baby skunks can't spray.* Skunks can spray to some extent within a few weeks after they're born, and can spray at full force at about three months old.

*Porcupines can shoot their quills.* Porcupines do not have ballistic quills. (But they are capable of thwacking predators with their tails.) If you touch a porcupine, its sharp quills may penetrate your skin and separate from the animal. The quills possess microscopic barbs on the tips that make them extremely difficult and painful to remove.

*Bears can hoot.* Black bear cubs moan, coo, mew, purr, bawl, and make gulping sounds. Adults grunt, bellow, and woof. On rare occasions, such as when cornered, bears growl. But they don't hoot. Owls hoot.

*If a tree falls in a forest and there is no one around to hear, it makes no sound.* Maybe. Maybe not. You're on your own for this one.

# Stellar among the Stars

## CIRCUMPOLAR CONSTELLATIONS

THERE WAS A TIME when it was always winter. Deep snow covered all but the treetops and animals were starving. Fisher, who was one of the most powerful animals, journeyed to Skyland to bring warm weather to Earth. With help from Wolverine, Fisher chewed a hole into Skyland. Warmth flowed down through the opening, melting the snow and causing flowers to bloom on Earth. When the Sky People discovered their warm weather was being stolen, they chased Fisher and cornered him atop a tall tree. One of their arrows struck the tip of Fisher's tail and he fell. But Fisher had made such a great sacrifice to help the animals that Creator gave him a place of honor among the stars.

In this Anishinabe (Ojibwa) story of How Fisher Went to Skyland, which comes from the Great Lakes region, the stars known widely as the Big Dipper instead take the form of a "fisher" or "fisher cat"—a fox-sized animal in the weasel family that has chocolate-brown fur and is a voracious hunter. The Big Dipper—one of the most recognizable images in the night sky—is a group of stars or *asterism*. It is formed from the same stars that mark the tail and rump of the constellation of the Great Bear, Ursa Major.

The two stars that form the outer rim of the Big Dipper's bowl can be used to find the North Star, Polaris. Draw an imaginary line from the star (Merak) at the bottom corner of the bowl and up through the star (Dubhe) along the rim. Follow that direction for about five times the distance between the "pointer stars" to locate Polaris.

The North Star forms the tip of the tail of the Little Bear, Ursa Minor,

which is also known as the Little Dipper. Because Polaris is positioned almost exactly above Earth's north pole, it appears stationary while all the other stars seem to revolve around it. This puts the seven stars that form the shape of the Little Dipper at the heart of the *circumpolar constellations*—those mythological images that circle the North Star and are high enough in the sky to be seen year-round. Other circumpolar constellations include Ursa Major, Draco (the Dragon), Cassiopeia (the Queen) and Cepheus (the King).

According to Greek mythology, Cassiopeia—queen and wife of King Cepheus—boasted of being more beautiful even than Juno, the wife (and sister) of Jupiter. When word of Cassiopeia's conceit reached Neptune, god of the sea, he dispatched a sea monster to attack the coast. Neptune demanded that Cepheus and Cassiopeia sacrifice their daughter, Andromeda, in order to stop the sea monster, but Perseus killed the creature and won Andromeda's hand in marriage.

A veritable theater of legends plays out across the twinkling arch of the night sky. Of the eighty-eight modern constellations, forty-one can be seen from the Northern Hemisphere. Except for the circumpolars, the other constellations are only visible seasonally. The folklore and traditional calendars of many indigenous peoples are inspired by the seasonal changes and nightly movements of the stars.

One Paiute legend from the Great Basin region of the western states, tells of a mountain sheep named Na-gah who wanted to make his father proud by climbing a tall mountain. But the slopes were so precipitous that every trail ended in a sheer cliff. The only route to the summit was a steep tunnel that wound up through the heart of the mountain. As Na-gah climbed, he dislodged boulders that rolled down and blocked the tunnel below. When he reached the mountaintop, it was just a small plateau from which he could not escape. At that moment Na-gah's father, Shinoh—a powerful being—was traveling across the sky and saw that Na-gah would die atop the mountain. Shinoh was so proud that he transformed Na-gah into a star and placed him in the center of the sky. To this day, all the other animals are circling Na-gah, still trying to climb the winding trails up that mountain to reach the summit.

If Na-gah's mountaintop were viewed overhead from a great distance, it would appear flat, with Na-gah in the center and all of the other animals circling around him. Similarly, from our vantage point on Earth, the stars are so distant that the dome of the night sky seems two-dimensional. Stars that appear to be close together are, in fact, separated from our home planet by vast distances. Among the stars of the Big Dipper, for example, Alioth is closest (70 light years away) and Alkaid is farthest (210 light years).

My favorite circumpolar is Draco, the Dragon. In Greek legend, Draco watches over the Golden Fleece sought by Jason and the Argonauts. In another tale, in the midst of the battle between the Titans and the gods of Mount Olympus, Athena flings the dragon heavenward where it wraps around the North Star. To this day, Draco's sinuous body and starry scales slither among the other circumpolars as if entrapping them in his celestial lair.

# Nature's Secret Codes

## FASCINATING FIBONACCIS

AVID SUMMER READERS immerse themselves in thrillers, pot-boilers, and fantasies whose plots swirl around sleuthing and solving mysterious codes. But look beyond the printed page, and you will quickly discover evidence of secret numbers hidden in the elegant patterns and intricate designs of nature itself.

In March 2005, I was flying to a book conference in Michigan when I looked out the window of the plane at the expanse of Lake Erie. Excited by what I saw, I wanted to stand and yell, "Look, everybody, isn't that amazing?!" Down below, the springtime ice-out had begun. Cracks had created enormous plates of ice hundreds of feet wide, forming a giant jigsaw puzzle whose pieces were in the shapes of pentagons and hexagons.

Search for this pattern in nature, and you will find it everywhere, from the hexagonal cells of honeycomb and the angles in which soap bubbles fit together in a mass of foam, to the shapes of a giraffe's spots and the scales on the backs of turtles, lizards, snakes, and armadillos. Look for hexagons amid corn kernels on the cob, in the vertical columns of basalt that cooled from volcanic lava, and where newly divided living cells lend a spherical start to life.

Closely packed objects in nature often form six sides because hexagons create the least amount of surface compared to area when objects are crowded together, while still leaving no wasted space in between. But the objects that are in close relationship, such as kernels and scales, must form simultaneously in order to create hexagons, in which all of the interior angles are 120 degrees. Things that form haphazardly over time, such as ice floes and the cracked plates on a dried-up mud flat, result in an imperfect mix of hexagons, pentagons, and the odd square.

Unlike hexagons, pentagons do not meet evenly in space and so are not found in minerals, crystals, and other rigid molecular structures. You will never see a five-armed snowflake. But living things can grow more fluidly, so five-petaled flowers are common. Cut an apple across the equator and you will unveil the pentacle-shaped seed chamber, the result of pollination in a five-petaled flower typical of the rose family.

Spirals are some of the most intriguing and universal patterns in nature. The arrangements of scales on conifer cones form equiangular spirals, in which each line drawn out from the center crosses the lines of the spiral at the same angle. Similar designs can be found among the seed heads of sunflowers and daisies, flower-bud scales, flower-petal arrangements, artichoke leaves, and the growth patterns of palm-tree leaves and pineapples. The same numbers that underlie these geometric patterns are also behind the shape of the chambered nautilus and the curvature of horns in wild sheep.

Pick up a pinecone, or the seed head of a sunflower, and solve the mystery. Scales and seeds form in spiral patterns that curve out from the center and contain a particular number in each spiral. Look closely and you will notice that the spirals run both clockwise and counterclockwise.

Another spiral pattern is found in the arrangements of leaves and thorns on stems. Start with a particular leaf and move up the stem. Count the number of passes you make around the stem and also the number of leaves you go by before you find a leaf whose stem lies almost exactly over the one where you began. Create a fraction with the number of passes on top and the number of leaves on the bottom. Among apples and oaks, for example, you will pass twice around the stem and count five leaves, so this fraction is ⅖. In beech and hazelnut, it is ⅓.

What is the secret key? All of the numbers contained in these spirals are in the

*Fibonacci numbers abound in the patterns of nature.*

Fibonacci sequence, discovered by Leonardo Pisano (Fibonacci), a mathematician in Pisa, Italy, 800 years ago. Fibonacci numbers are calculated by starting with the number 1 and arriving at each subsequent number by adding the value of the last number in the sequence to the one that precedes it: 1, 1, 2, 3, 5, 8, 13, 21, 34, 55, and so on.

Pine needles always occur in bundles of 2, 3, or 5 (all Fibonaccis). The pentagon is a common Fibonacci in living things, appearing in the number of arms on a sea star, the patterns found on a sand dollar, in many flowers and fruits, and in the patterns formed by branches. Fibonacci numbers also show up in art, architecture, poetry, music, science, and technology.

Living things do not follow the code of Fibonacci numbers by design or calculation: they simply form patterns that create the most efficient spatial relationships. Fortunately for us, the geometry of Fibonaccis creates a world of natural beauty and visual poetry.

## How Much Wool Would
## a Woolly Bear, Bear?

I ONCE HAD A COLLEGE PROFESSOR who claimed he could predict the weather by playing woolly bears like dice. He would pick up a woolly bear, which immediately curled up, then shake the fuzz-ball, blow on it and roll it onto the ground. If the woolly uncurled and crept east or west, an average winter was coming. When it crawled north, mild weather lay ahead. But if it headed south, beware!

Across its vast range, which stretches from northern Mexico throughout the lower forty-eight states and up into southern Canada, the woolly bear has many names, including "banded woolly bear," "black-ended bear" or "woolly worm," as it is called in the South. Several myths are based on the three bands of a woolly's coat. Some say that a wide middle band is a harbinger of a mild winter. Others insist that if the black band in front is longer than the one in the rear, the early part of the coming winter will be more harsh, and vice versa. There's even a story that the number of body segments covered with black fuzz foretells the number of hard winter months ahead.

In truth, the woolly bear's stripes paint a picture of weather past. There are thirteen segments to a woolly bear's body: the front four to five segments are black, the middle four to six are reddish-brown, and the rear two to three segments are also black. Occasionally, all-black woollies have been found.

The woolly bear's reddish-brown band grows faster than the black bands on each end as the caterpillar ages. During mild autumn weather, the tawny middle grows quite wide before the larvae enter winter dormancy. Wide middle bands seen in autumn, or in the following spring, are evidence of a

lingering fall. During a cool autumn, however, woolly bears grow slowly, so the black bands tend to remain wider. If woolly bears are forced to hibernate when their black bands are still quite wide, it's because an early winter came along. Woolly bears found in the spring with narrow middle bands are a reminder that the past winter came early.

Why bear wool at all? A woolly's bristles do not sting, nor is its body poisonous. But the stiff hairs adhere to the stomach linings of birds and upset their digestive process, which discourages birds from eating them. Our native cuckoos are among the few local birds that can ingest woolly bears and other hairy caterpillars. (See "Of Cuckoos and Caterpillars.") Certain mammals may also partake, including deer mice, raccoons, coyotes, striped skunks, and red foxes.

Woolly bears feed in old fields, roadsides, pastures, and meadows. Although they prefer plantains, dandelions, and grasses, they will consume campions, clovers, asters, and other flowers. Woollies eat the lower leaves and do little or no damage to gardens and ornamentals. "The caterpillars do eat elms, maples, birches, sunflowers, and other species," says Donald Lewis, extension entomologist for Ohio State University and an expert on woollies, "but their population is never large enough to have a significant impact on foliage. And there aren't enough of them to have a big effect on nutrient cycling as they convert leaves into droppings."

The woollies we see in autumn are the summer's second generation. Caterpillars emerge in April or May, feed and then spin a brown cocoon of silk into which they weave a soft felt made of their own hairs. Cocoons are located in deeply furrowed tree bark, in rock crevices, and beneath stones. After pupating two weeks, an Isabella tiger moth emerges from the cocoon. Female Isabellas have orange-tinted wings, while the males' wings are tan. The abdomen is covered with a tawny felt bearing three rows of black spots.

Fertilized females lay pale yellow eggs on the leaves of plants that will make good food for the larvae. Eggs hatch a week later. Caterpillars molt about six times as they grow. With each new instar, the brownish, middle band widens. When this first generation of larvae matures, they pupate, transform into adult moths, and lay the eggs that will hatch into the crop of late-summer woollies.

As autumn progresses, woolly bears scurry in search of a cozy place to overwinter, marching intently across the landscape, seemingly unaware of the dangers they face on their final sojourn of the year. Woollies that encounter a busy roadway continue to creep apace, crossing with abandon. At those times, I try to slow down and avoid high-speed routes, doing what I can to honor the woollies' right of way.

Wintering woollies favor the shelter beneath leaves and under rocks and logs. Concentrated proteins and sugars in their body fluids form an antifreeze so effective that a caterpillar can even survive being encased in ice. But be careful if you discover a dormant woolly bear—the heat from your hand can cause it to thaw and awaken, at its peril.

# Phenomenal Phenology

OUR FICKLE NEW ENGLAND WEATHER often appears in daily discourse. When boasting about having endured one meteorological extreme or another, New Englanders can sometimes stretch the limits of credibility. One old-timer is reported to have buttonholed his neighbor with, "Last winter, the temperature outside my window dropped 50 degrees in 12 hours!"

To which the neighbor replied, "Yup, I used to have a thermometer just like that."

Yankee stoicism aside, global climate change is influencing our already tempestuous atmosphere. But how can we tell the difference between the normal ups and downs of local weather and the abnormal effects of global warming, especially when our "normal" weather fluctuations tend toward the extreme?

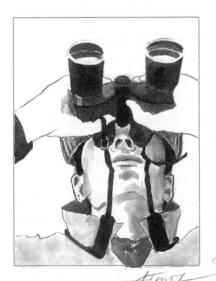

Short of becoming climate scientists, one way for each of us to track climate change is to observe and carefully record how plants and animals respond to the seasons over time. When do the redwinged blackbirds return in the springtime? What date marks the first run of maple sap? How soon do the lilacs bloom? On which autumn morning will we discover the first glistening frost of the season?

Keeping track of natural events and cycles is called *phenology*—a word that comes from the Greek *phainestain*, "to appear," and *logos*, "study." You can become a phenologist simply by maintaining a detailed record of how temperature, light, and precipitation affect the life cycles of local plants and animals from year to year.

Some famous phenologists include Carl Linnaeus, Henry David Thoreau, John Muir, Aldo Leopold, and Reverend Gilbert White of Selborne, England. Thoreau created a detailed calendar of events for the natural history of Concord, Massachusetts. He charted the progress of plants and animals through the seasons during a ten-year period that ended in 1861, including the dates when birds returned in the springtime, when insects hatched, when flowers bloomed, and when leaf buds unfurled. Thoreau's phenological records, and their relevance to today's changing climate, are the subject of *Walden Warming: Climate Change Comes to Thoreau's Woods*, by Richard B. Primack.

In his landmark book on conservation, *A Sand County Almanac*, Aldo Leopold chronicled the natural world over time. Between 1935 and 1945 he made careful annual records of 145 natural events in Madison, Wisconsin—work that is still being carried on by his descendants. Leopold once noted that, "In June as many as a dozen species may burst their buds on a single day."

I confess to being an intermittent phenologist. One of the lists I've kept includes dates for when the first hummingbirds appear at our Vermont feeders: 5/28/92 and 5/29/93 (South Pomfret); 5/22/95, 5/13/96, 5/13/97, and 5/15/98 (Union Village); and 5/8/03, 5/11/04, 5/15/05, and 5/7/07 (Chester). While this record is incomplete and varies geographically, it does show how consistent hummingbird arrivals can be in any one location, and it documents that hummingbirds arrive later in northern locales and at higher elevations.

Knowledge of the timing of natural events is crucial for nursery growers, farmers, gardeners, and others who rely on seasonal events such as maple sugaring, leaf peeping, or skiing. Consistent records are invaluable for tracking the health of ecosystems, documenting changes in populations, and marking the distribution patterns of plants and animals. Information about the hatches of disease-carrying insects and ticks can help experts monitor and predict the steady march northward of threats to public health such as West Nile virus (mosquitoes) and Lyme disease (deer ticks).

In our society, where people move an average of every five years, it is difficult to amass a meaningful body of natural history observations through time. But you can still make your observations count by entering the information into an online database called the USA National Phenology Network (www.usanpn.org).

The next time the season begins to turn, you can use it as an opportunity to contribute to the collective understanding of how the natural world, influenced by human activities, is changing over time. Simply choose the aspects of plant and animal life that truly interest you and keep detailed, timely annual accounts. Lilac flowers, for example, are an excellent indicator. Following exposure to an essential period of winter chill, lilacs respond by blooming in a very predictable way when the warm days of springtime arrive.

Observations are best if recorded in the same place each year by the same individual, since this allows for the most meaningful comparisons through time. If enough people keep accurate journals of natural events in their own backyards—including dates and observations—this national database will create a picture of nature's seasonal changes across the continent, providing scientists with vital information for studying global climate change and shifts in local weather.

Over the years, I've developed an appreciation for how our neighbors in the natural world can endure the ever-increasing extremes of seasonal weather in the North Country. Mark Twain got it right when he described New England weather: "There is only one thing certain about it; you are certain there is going to be plenty of it."

# HARVESTS
# & HUNTS

# Eat Your Weedies

## STALKING THE BACKYARD BUFFET

IN THE EARLY 1960S, Euell Gibbons wrote *Stalking the Wild Asparagus* and introduced millions of North Americans to the virtues of harvesting wild foods. Many of Gibbons' devotees were descended from ancestors who regularly supplemented their diet with wild mushrooms, roots, berries, and nuts. Gibbons' book was a revelation that showed how to rediscover the tradition of foraging for meals from among the plants that grow nearby.

Since that time, gathering wild edibles has become increasingly popular and, in our region, woods-grown delicacies such as ramps and fiddlehead ferns appear in grocery stores each spring. Yet you don't have to lace up your hiking boots to enjoy the wild repast. If you resist the urge to use herbicides and pesticides, the keys to unlocking the taste sensations and nutritional values of a diverse array of edible wild plants are waiting in your lawn and vegetable garden.

Let's start with that botanical Darth Vader in the eyes of lawn perfectionists—the *dent de lion*, "lion's tooth," or dandelion (*Taraxacum officinale*), so named for the tooth-like serrations on its leaves. Pick the young leaves for salad greens early in the season, before the flowers bloom and the leaves become bitter. Use blossoms to make dandelion wine or batter-fried fritters. Dig the roots, clean them, and slow roast until crisp, then grind and brew into a caffeine-free coffee substitute.

In striking contrast is the sharp, peppery taste of a wild mustard called winter cress, or garden yellow rocket (*Barbarea vulgaris*)—among the first plants to sprout after snowmelt. The leaves add character to any salad, but I

Dandelion.

prefer them steamed like domestically grown mustard greens, or added to soups.

Nearby, you'll likely find red clover (*Trifolium pratense*) and white clover (*T. repens*). As with the dandelion, these clovers originally came from Europe. The leaves are good for salads and can be boiled for five to ten minutes for cooked greens. Crush the dried leaves into bread dough to enhance the leavening of yeast.

Common sheep sorrel (*Rumex acetosella*) is another strong-flavored herb whose fleshy, arrow-shaped leaves add bite to a salad. Or boil the fresh leaves to create a tart tea, which can be chilled and sweetened for a lemonade-like cooler that's loaded with vitamin C. The shamrock-shaped leaves of the violet wood-sorrel (*Oxalis violacea*) and common wood-sorrel (*Oxalis acetosella*) can be similarly prepared.

As springtime progresses, look for the heart-shaped leaves of wild violets (*Viola spp.*).

When violets bloom in our own lawn, they create such a rich carpet of blue and white that I cease mowing those spots for several weeks. Especially good when young and tender, the leaves make an excellent salad green or potherb that is high in vitamins A and C. Violets can be eaten freshly picked, or the boiled leaves can be used as a thickener in soups. Beware the leaves of yellow violets, however, which have a laxative effect.

Search the unkempt margins of the yard and you'll notice the scalloped leaves of oxeye daisy (*Leucanthemum vulgare*), another European immigrant. These leaves, with their pleasant, slightly spicy taste, make a tender garnish or salad green.

Flowerbeds and vegetable gardens often harbor two species that are among our most common edible "weeds"—lamb's quarters or pigweed (*Chenopodium album*) and purslane (*Portulaca oleracea*). Pick the thick, arrow-shaped leaves of lamb's quarters, which are coated with a whitish bloom, when the plant is less than a foot high. Boil or steam the leaves lightly, then serve with butter

*Edible "weeds" (left to right): dandelion,
lamb's quarters (pigweed), and purslane.*

and thyme for a spinach-like dish that is rich in vitamins A and C, as well as
B-complex vitamins, calcium, iron, and phosphorous. Lamb's quarters taste
so good you'll wonder why you're not growing the plant on purpose, rather
than treating it as a weed. The fleshy leaves of purslane, which often grows
near lamb's quarters, can also be eaten in salads, or you can boil them for ten
minutes as a tart, tasty potherb. Purslane is used to thicken soups, and some
people enjoy pickling the stems.

After your lawn has gone feral, the tiny, five-petaled white flowers of wild
strawberry (*Fragaria virginiana*) may appear, harbingers of the miniature,
ruby-colored confections to come. The sweet scent and flavor of these minute
gems put domesticated varieties to shame. You have to pick a lot of them
because they're so small, but they're worth the time and effort. Try baking
them into muffins or pancakes, or sprinkling them on your cereal, over fresh
yogurt, or into homemade ice cream. Create wild strawberry jam.

As the season progresses into summer, your reward for maintaining a chemical-free lawn and garden will be a succession of useful ripening plants—from the fragrant, chamomile-like blossoms of pineapple weed (*Matricaria discoidea*), to the snappy seeds of jewelweed (*Impatiens capensis* and *I. pallida*), which taste like walnuts. And you'll be joined by a host of birds, bees, butterflies, and other wildlife that come to partake of the abundant nectar, leaves, fruits, and seeds offered up in the wild harvest.

# Hunting with the Abenaki

## INDIGENOUS WILDLIFE MANAGEMENT

SINCE LONG BEFORE EUROPEANS began building permanent set-
tlements in the Northeast over 400 years ago, an indigenous culture who
call themselves *Alnôbak*, "The People," have inhabited a broad region now
defined by Vermont, New Hampshire, Quebec, and neighboring Maine and
Massachusetts. Today their descendants, who are also known as the *Abenaki*,
"People of the Dawn," still refer to their homeland as *Kedakina*, "Our Land."

In popular misconception, the Alnôbak of lore lived in an unbroken wil-
derness, hunting and gathering and making use of whatever abundance they
could find. The reality, as evidenced from archeological digs, historical records,
and cultural memory, is far more complex and interesting.

With the coming of autumn—a time of year known as *Penibagos kisos*,
the "leaf-falling moon"—hunters left their homesites near summer gardens
and traveled to the uplands and northern parts of the home range to seasonal
hunting lodges. Using intimate knowledge of deer and other game, the hunters
baited trap lines and strung them for several miles. Hunters used knives, bows
and arrows, spears, snares, pitfall traps, and the *kelahigan*—deadfall trap—a
heavy log that dropped and crushed an animal's skull when it tried to snatch
the bait underneath.

Deer, bear, and moose were the greatest sources of winter protein among
the Alnôbak, together with beaver, raccoon, bobcat, woodchuck, porcupine,
cottontail, gray and red fox, skunk, red and gray squirrel, muskrat, chipmunk, mouse, and even shrew. Other wild prey were taken when and where
they could be found, including elk, turkey, otter, wolf, marten, lynx, ruffed

grouse, spruce grouse, snapping turtle, hooded and common merganser, and migratory birds such as the passenger pigeon, Canada goose, and a variety of other waterfowl. Meat was cut into strips, dried and smoked by hanging on lodgepoles or draping over racks by the fire.

In the northern and middle regions of Kedakina, hunters and their dogs commonly stalked white-tailed deer individually. To the south, up the river valleys and along the coast, hunters sometimes lit a fire, *skweda*, and burned brush to drive deer and other game animals into funnel-shaped enclosures where hunters lay in wait. Animals were snared or shot with arrows as they pressed through the narrow opening.

The Alnôbak also purposefully cleared land close to villages to enhance wildlife habitat. Hunters noticed that deer, elk, cottontail, and other prey frequented the openings formed when a forest was felled by a blowdown, burned by a lightning fire, or transformed into a wet meadow above a beaver dam. Animals were drawn to the fresh growth that sprouted when the understory was exposed to sunlight—grasses, greens, berries, and the buds of shrubs and young trees.

*Setting the* kelahigan *or "deadfall trap."*

Stone knives and axes were used to girdle tree bark and kill sections of forest. Dead trees were then burned on the stump. This land-use pattern created an expansive mosaic of habitats in various stages of growth, ranging from fresh clearings to mature forest—a landscape of diverse food and cover that attracted many game animals. Families moved when the habitat and animal populations needed time to recover and replenish.

In fire, the Alnôbak employed an immensely powerful ally. In addition to creating garden sites and improving wildlife habitat, fires were lit in the spring and autumn to encourage the emergence of berries and other foods. Fires also enlarged the size of grasslands, making it easier to see who, friend or foe, was approaching a village. Burned areas freed of underbrush were easier to travel through, harbored fewer biting insects, and made animals more visible near the *Alnigamigol*, or wigwams. Regular burning also prevented larger fires from spreading into the village or reaching the tree crowns and causing an intense conflagration. Signal fires and smoke were used to communicate across long distances.

As time passed, regular burning formed large intervales along the river-banks. The once-abundant heath hen (now extinct) lived in expansive, prai-rie-like grasslands of up to a few hundred acres each that were created along the coast as far north as southern Maine. After woodland bison crossed the Mississippi, some 1,000 years ago, the park-like forests and wide grasslands also attracted these grazing animals into southern New England.

Each Alnôbak family had a specific territory under its care and protection where they closely observed the plants and animals. Hunters could tell which animals were weak or healthy, which were young or old, and even whether or not a doe was pregnant. They watched the number of animals carefully and hunted so as to maintain strong breeding populations. Archaeologists have discovered that some families hunted mostly male white-tailed deer: the remains of meals at some ancient homesites are nearly devoid of bones from female deer.

Wasteful killing was not condoned among the Alnôbak, nor is it considered acceptable among the Abenaki today. Among those who still follow the old traditions, hunting is considered both a way of survival and an expression of how well The People respect the life around them. Within this belief system animals have their own individual lives, families, and spirits. Similar to humans, animals form communities and cultures with their own fates and destinies.

Each year, when the leaf-falling moon is upon us, hunters across the region still make their way to seasonal game camps in the uplands, as they have for millennia here in Kedakina.

# Scrumptious Seaweeds

## GASTRONOMIC DELIGHTS

## OF THE THALLOPHYTES

I GREW UP DOWN THE ROAD from a village named Apponaug that is perched at the head of a cove branching off Narragansett Bay. *Apponaug* is the Narragansett Indian word for "the place where shellfish are roasted." In the Wampanoag language it means "seafood cooking" or "clambake," referring to the traditional meal in which corn, lobsters, and clams—along with potatoes, onions, and sometimes other foods—are steamed on a bed of seaweed heated by hot round rocks set in a circular hole in the ground.

The seaweed used by the Wampanoag and Narragansett peoples then and now is a kind of brown algae called rockweed (*Ascophyllum nodosum*). Today, it and many other seaweeds are growing in popularity and increasingly appreciated as foods that are rich in essential amino acids, vitamins, and nutrients. Seaweeds are also harvested for use as an organic fertilizer.

New England's miles of coastline are festooned with seaweeds, but we rarely eat these nutritious algae unless they are wrapped around a dollop of sushi or used as thickeners (alginates and carrageenan) in our milkshakes, ice cream, cheese, and yogurt. In addition to being high in potassium, iodine, vitamin B-12, and other essential nutrients and trace minerals, seaweed is rich in protein and "brain food"—omega-3 fatty acids. Not only is it good for you, seaweed also lends unique textures to foods and enhances the flavors and aromas of companion ingredients in many dishes.

Cultivating seaweed is also good for the environment. An article by Dana Goodyear in the November 2, 2015, issue of the *New Yorker* refers to seaweed

Atlantic wakame
(Alaria esculenta).

as "one of the world's most sustainable and nutritious crops." As it grows, seaweed absorbs the phosphorous and nitrogen that enters oceans from agricultural runoff and wastewater treatment plants. An excess of these nutrients can cause great blooms of algae. When those algae die and decompose, oxygen is depleted to the point where few plants or animals can survive. Growing seaweed also absorbs carbon dioxide, a critical cause of global climate change as well as ocean acidification, which is harmful to marine plants and animals, especially coral reefs. So consuming seaweed enables us to have our carbon, and eat it, too.

In addition to being an Earth-friendly endeavor, foraging for edible seaweeds offers both instant gratification and opportunities for preparing nutritionally sound epicurean delights to enrich the palate. Much of the enjoyment lies in the adventure of gathering seaweed itself—the unexpected encounters and new discoveries on a quiet seaside stroll. Here are a few of the most common edible seaweeds along our coastline. Beyond these simple suggestions, you can find many seaweed recipes online.

## BROWN SEAWEED

## Edible Kelp

The two most commonly eaten brown algae are sugar kelp (*Saccharina latissima*) and Atlantic wakame (*Alaria esculenta*). *Alaria* derives from the Latin for "wing," while *esculenta* means "edible." Both have dark brown, flowing blades of 5 to 10 feet long. (The pliable blades of sugar kelp somewhat resemble giant lasagna noodles.) Atlantic wakame grows at the low-tide mark, and sugar kelp can be found in the zone just below the low-tide mark. Gather *Alaria* in the summer months when fresh bunches of the frayed blades wash ashore after a storm. The sporophylls, or small side-shoots that come off the stipe (main stalk), are the most tender and delicious parts of the plant. Chop and sauté fresh *Alaria* into a vegetable stir-fry or add directly to soups and salads. As it cooks it turns green and imbues the dish with its own subtly earthy flavor. *Alaria* and *Saccharina* can both be dried, powdered, and used as seasonings that are especially good on vegetables.

## RED SEAWEEDS

## Nori and Laver (*Porphyra* species)

Several species of East Coast seaweed—ranging from about 6 to 12 inches long and from dull-red to rosy—can be made into nori or laver. The delicate, ruffled blades of laver are translucent. Look for them in the upper tide zone just as the tide starts to go out. As you gather the blades try rinsing one off and nibbling it, for laver is fairly tender right from the sea. Then wash the blades you've collected, steam them for a few minutes until tender, and eat them like a vegetable, or chop and add them to soups. Laver can also be dried and stored for later use. To prepare a marine version of stuffed grape leaves, use fresh laver fronds as a substitute for *Vitus*; if using dried laver, boil the fronds for about a minute to make them pliable before wrapping around the stuffing.

## Dulse (*Palmaria palmata*)

Like a purplish-red drape, dulse hangs upside down, growing up to 1 foot long at the lowest edge of the low-tide zone and down into deeper water. As the species name suggests, dulse is lobed or "palmate" in shape. Once dulse is dried, its rubbery texture becomes paper-like and translucent. In this form it can be crumbled over salads as a flavor accent or eaten as a kind of seaweed roll-up—a convenient trailside snack. The salty flavor is especially satisfying

when consumed on a hot day, and it replenishes essential minerals that are lost through sweating. Dulse is commonly used as a source of iodine to help people who suffer from gout.

## Irish Moss (*Chondrus crispus*)

The flattened, branching blades of Irish moss are a purplish-red color but can shimmer with a beautiful bluish tint when submerged. It can grow up to 6 inches long near the bottom of the low tide zone. Although very tough when fresh, it quickly softens after being boiled or steamed for just a few minutes. Use Irish moss to thicken soups by cutting it up and dropping it into the boiling broth for about half an hour. Keep boiling beyond the soup stage and you will end up with jelly: Irish moss contains a gelling agent called carrageenan. Used in products as varied as pharmaceuticals, toothpaste, ice cream, and cheese, carrageenan is one of the most ubiquitous substances derived from seaweed. However, Irish moss is probably best known as the base for making blancmange. An excellent recipe for this dish can be found in Euell Gibbons' *Stalking the Blue-eyed Scallop*.

## Sea Lettuce (*Ulva lactuca*)

Search in the low tidal zone of brackish waters for sea lettuce's shiny green, ruffled, translucent sheets up to 1 foot long. When cooked, the tough, rubbery blades become tender. Boil or stir-fry sea lettuce with vegetables for no more than ten minutes. Sea lettuce, either raw or cooked, makes a hardy addition to salads and soups. Some like to wrap it around fish filets before frying them. When dried and powdered, sea lettuce becomes a salty salad seasoning.

### GATHERING, PRESERVING, AND PREPARING EDIBLE SEAWEEDS

#### Safety

+ Be certain of a seaweed's identity. *If you're not sure what it is, don't eat it.*
+ Pick seaweeds growing in waters that are at least clean enough for fishing. Don't pick seaweed growing in water that is near areas that are sprayed with chemicals, or in water near storm drains or sewage treatment plant outflows.
+ Learn how to identify poison ivy, oak, and sumac so that you can avoid them when foraging along the shoreline.
+ Beware broken glass, discarded cans, and other hazards.

#### Gathering and Preserving Seaweed

+ Gather seaweeds safely, at low tide.
+ Clean the seaweed with salt water, which helps preserve it. Do not rinse it with fresh water until you are ready to prepare it for eating.

- Place in a plastic bag or some other airtight container.
- Put the seaweed on ice and, once home, place it in the refrigerator.
- Please respect the seaweeds that you pick. In some places certain species are endangered because of widespread harvesting. The Abenaki, and other indigenous peoples, traditionally collect only from abundant growths of seaweed and leave many behind to replenish the stand. The largest "grandmother" in a patch is not picked, nor are seaweeds that are rare or scarce. It is customary to give thanks to the seaweed and the Creator for the gifts they bestow.

## Preparing Seaweed

- Be certain of the proper way to prepare the seaweed so that it is safe to eat.
- Just before preparing your seaweed, wash it gently but thoroughly with lukewarm water to remove sand and grit. Then rinse in cool water.
- If you want to dry your seaweed in order to store it for later use, wash it well as described above. You can air-dry the seaweed in a warm, sunny, well-ventilated outdoor space by laying the blades on a dry towel or hanging them from a clothesline. Simply turn the blades once in a while to allow for even drying on all sides. Dry them inside by placing the blades on a sheet pan, warming in a 200-degree Fahrenheit oven for about 15 minutes on one side, turning the blade over, then warming for another 15 minutes. Release the moisture by leaving the oven door slightly ajar.
- Place dried seaweed in airtight containers and store in a dark, well-ventilated place, *not in the refrigerator*. If you are preparing soup or some other watery dish, dried seaweed can be dropped right in. Otherwise, you will need to soak the dried blades in water before adding them to your recipe.

# Herps in the Garden

## SNAKES AND TOADS

## PROVIDE PEST CONTROL

WHILE BASKING IN THE LUXURIANCE of our summer garden, we often feel like we're in our own little Eden. When the first fruits of the season ripen, however, we don't need a serpent to tempt us into taking that first juicy bite. Instead, the morality plays overheard amid the garden rows are more often concerned with how to manage the pest-of-the-day with biological controls, while resisting the temptation to use chemicals. Cultivated gardens can be sustainable if growing practices are aligned with the cycles of nature. A balanced relationship between predators and prey is essential. Snakes and toads are critical links in the garden food chain.

Encountering a snake in the garden causes many people to shriek or even panic. Yet snakes and another often unloved creature, the American toad, are among the most effective forms of pest control. If you tolerate these herpetological visitors—or better yet, encourage their presence—you'll be less likely to share your garden with ravenous bugs, or bottles of pesticide.

Several kinds of snakes make themselves at home in local gardens. The common garter snake is identifiable by the three yellow stripes running along its back. In my garden, this snake often suns itself between rows of vegetables, absorbing heat while digesting slugs, caterpillars, sowbugs, and other garden pests. Larger garter snakes (they can grow to about 3 feet long) also eat meadow voles, which will otherwise wreak havoc on roots, tubers, and bark.

My favorite snakes are among the most docile encountered in a garden: the smooth green snake and the ring-necked snake. The grass-hued scales of the

green snake blend in well. Almost three-fourths of its diet consists of insects, including grasshoppers, hornworms, and other crop-munching caterpillars. The ring-necked snake, named for its golden collar, stalks similar prey, but it does so under the stars. With a back the color of night, and its bright yellow belly pressed to the earth, it's well camouflaged for nocturnal hunting.

In contrast, the ornery milk snake strikes when threatened. Although nonvenomous, the milk snake's attitude, size (it grows to 3 feet long) and rows of alternating reddish-brown splotches—not unlike the patterning of a copperhead or timber rattlesnake—have earned it an undeserved reputation and the misnomer of "adder." In fact, it is harmless to all but the mice, voles, other small mammals, and other snakes that comprise up to 70 percent of its diet.

You can attract snakes to your garden by providing habitat: loose rock piles, brush piles, prone boards, stacks of wood, and unkempt corner swales. And since pesticides can sicken and kill reptiles and amphibians (which can absorb toxins directly through the skin), maintaining a chemical-free garden safeguards these natural predators.

Most snakes consume far more garden pests than they do beneficial species. Unfortunately, larger snakes do prey on that superhero of herpetological pest control: the American toad, which can devour three times its own weight in bugs per day. One toad can eat 50 to 100 insects and other prey each night, or 10,000 in a growing season. More than 80 percent of their diet consists of harmful garden pests, including slugs, earwigs, Japanese beetles, cutworms, grasshoppers, sow bugs, snails, cucumber beetles, grubs, and tent caterpillars.

In the children's story *The Wind in the Willows*, Toad lives on an historic estate with all of the modern conveniences. In real life, toads require only a cool, moist environment. They frequently take cover under mulch or hide in the undergrowth of a feral garden corner. To avoid the desiccating heat of the sun, they're most active during the evening and at night (particularly wet nights). When toads like their habitat, they'll remain for a year or more and simply dig a deeper burrow to overwinter. If you happen to touch a toad while working in the garden, don't be concerned: despite the old tales, toads do not cause warts.

It's easy to construct your own Toad Hall. Place a terra-cotta pot upside down in a shady nook with a thin layer of leaves for bedding. Dig a tunnel about 3 inches wide and 3 inches deep so toads can creep in under the rim of the pot. The clay pot absorbs rainwater, which evaporates and cools the interior.

Toads are also drawn to water, so you might build a tiny pond to complement your toad home. Set a birdbath into the earth so that the lip is level with the ground, or dig an 8- to 12-inch deep depression that measures 3 to 4 feet across and is partly shaded. Since toads can't climb out of a pond if the edge is steep, make sure one side slopes down gently. Line the hole with plastic. Create a small patch of gravel on part of the bottom and spread a thin layer of mud over the rest where dragonflies and damselflies can lay their eggs; the nymphs will hatch into adults that eat lots of garden pests (and, in the meantime, will prey on any mosquito larvae). Don't add fish or red-spotted newts to the pond or they'll eat everything else.

It only takes a little encouragement to attract beneficial herps to your garden. Even if your relationship with snakes doesn't progress beyond mutual tolerance, toads do tend to grow on you.

# Wild Nuts

## AUTUMN BOUNTY, HOLIDAY TREAT

GATHERING WILD NUTS is an autumn rite for many families and a longstanding tradition among the Western Abenaki. Historically, when garden soil became depleted and villages were moved to new ground, piles of acorns, butternuts, chestnuts, black walnuts, hazelnuts, and others were placed around the new home site. Squirrels gathered this largess and buried the nuts in secret caches. Stores that were forgotten grew into orchard-like groves of "wild" nuts around the lodges.

From hickory nuts to acorns, hazelnuts to black walnuts, nut-bearing trees and shrubs produce a wild harvest for anyone who wants to forage and live off the land. Local wild nuts are free and healthy to eat. Plus, they don't require burning carbon-emitting fuels to produce the crops and transport them from growers thousands of miles away. Wild nuts are organic, unless someone has sprayed chemicals on local trees and shrubs. And it's fun to gather them with family and friends.

Walnuts have been called ambrosia—food of the gods. The genus name, *Juglans*, comes from the Latin, *Jovis glans*, meaning "Jupiter's acorns." In ancient lore, it was said that people dined on acorns, but Jupiter, the Roman deity of the sky, ate walnuts. In fact, black walnuts are superior sources of nutrition, being 25 percent protein and rich in omega-3, polyunsaturated fats, which current research suggests may promote heart health, decrease the incidence of certain cancers, enhance memory function, and reduce the risk of arthritis.

Black walnut (*Juglans nigra*) prefers the rich, moist woodlands of central and southern states; in the Northeast this sun-loving tree grows mostly where planted in parks, backyards, and village greens and along roadsides. A close relative, butternut or white walnut (*Juglans cinerea*), once grew throughout the northern woodlands; sadly, this species has been decimated by a canker disease.

Walnuts have a thick, spongy green husk with a sticky coat. Inside is a stubborn shell that requires a nutcracker, hammer, or rock to open. I once met a black-walnut aficionado who folded the nuts into a sheet on his driveway and ran over them with his car. Nutmeats can be boiled to extract the oil, or they can be ground to make a rich-tasting meal. But don't keep the nutmeats for more than a few weeks or they will become rancid. They can be stored for a few months if refrigerated, and longer if frozen.

Hickory nuts produce a generous yield (one pound of nutmeats from two pounds of nuts) for far less work with a nutcracker. The sweetest nuts come from mockernut hickory (*Carya tomentosa*) and shagbark hickory (*Carya ovata*), so named for its large, peeling plates of bark. Each husk encloses a thick shell around a tasty nut. Eat them out of hand or substitute them for walnuts when cooking. Nuts of the bitternut hickory (*Carya cordiformis*) and pignut hickory (*Carya glabra*) are not as tasty, as their names imply.

Oak trees commonly grow alongside hickories. Acorns from the white oak group, whose leaves have rounded lobes and tips—including white oak,

*Abenaki birch-bark bucket with nuts.*

swamp oak, and chestnut oak—are best for eating. Trees in the black oak group—such as black oak, red oak, and scarlet oak with their sharp-tipped leaves—produce acorns with too much bitter tannin.

Gather acorns from the eastern white oak (*Quercus alba*) soon after they fall, remove the shells and drop them into a pot of boiling water for 15 to 20 minutes until the water turns brown. Drain and repeat, then put the nuts in a well-ventilated place to dry. Roast the dried nuts at 300 degrees for about an hour, then eat them plain or grind them into a flour-like meal to be used in bread-baking. Acorn bread is still baked in southern Italy and many cultures use acorns for high-protein fodder.

One of our most prolific nut-bearing trees, American beech (*Fagus grandifolia*), has the misfortune of being sheathed in smooth bark that is sometimes used as a carving post, a practice that exposes the tree's interior to infection and disease. In fact, the word *beech* comes from the Anglo-Saxon *boc*, meaning "word" or "letter," and from which "book" is derived. Prior to papyrus, beech

## Nuts of New England

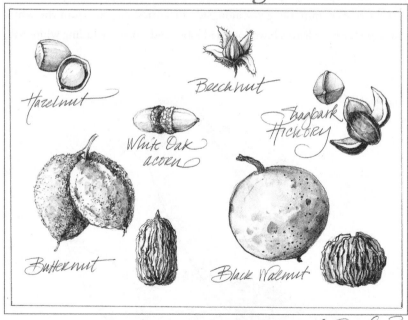

bark was harvested as sheets for writing tablets. A stylus pushed over the bark tracked along the straight lines of grain, so circles had to be formed as a graduated series of corners. Thus, Gothic writing evolved as letters composed of angles, rather than curves.

You have to be quick to harvest beechnuts because birds, deer, and squirrels devour them almost as soon as they ripen (or stash them in stone walls, holes, or hollow logs in preparation for lean winter months). Beech trees bear nuts annually, setting a heavy crop every third year. Two to three, ¾-inch triangular nuts nestle inside each bristle-covered husk. After removing the nuts, roast them at 350 degrees for about five minutes, then cool and eat out of hand. They also can be processed in a small cider press to obtain the oil, or dried and ground into flour.

Our local hazelnuts, which are closely related to European filberts, are steeped in the traditional folklore of Europe and colonial America. A young woman would name individual hazelnuts after the men she was attracted to. When she threw the hazelnuts onto the glowing coals of the hearth, the name associated with the nut that flared brightest was destined to become her "fate" in marriage. Perhaps this is why we still say that the object of someone's affection is their "flame."

One must also hurry to gather hazelnuts, because squirrels and mice quickly consume or add them to their winter middens. American hazelnut (*Corylus americana*) grows to 8 feet tall in hedgerows and moist woodlands. The nuts of beaked hazelnut (*Corylus cornuta*) sport a protuberance at the top of the husk. The ripe nuts, gathered in September, have thin shells and sweet meats. The nutmeats, fortunately, separate easily from the shell. They can be eaten raw, roasted, or ground into flour, and are an excellent source of potassium.

When the holidays arrive, consider wild nuts as a wholesome and delicious treat. Try using black walnut meats in turkey stuffing, in meatless casseroles, or when making cakes, cookies, and fudge. For a holiday cookie, find a recipe for "pecan sandies" and substitute ground hazelnuts or black walnuts for the pecan meal. And, since children love to crack nuts open and eat them, drop a handful of hazelnuts into their gifts of the season.

OUT OF
BALANCE

# Whither Fall Foliage
## in an Age of Climate Change

THE ALLURE OF FALL FOLIAGE draws millions of travelers to the winding back roads of New England, where trees display such a spectacle that even
the most jaded traveler stops to gape open-mouthed at the astonishing colors.
Half of the states in the nation rely on some form of foliage-season tourism
income, but "leaf-peeping" in northern New England is an annual pilgrimage
that generates well over $2 billion. So when talk turns to how foliage is being
impacted by climate change, people listen.

In 2014 the displays of leaf color in Maine, New Hampshire, and Vermont
were particularly deep and vibrant. This followed several years of notably
pastel autumn coloration during which the leaves turned mostly from green
to brown before they dropped. With autumn color so variable, how can the
long-term effects of climate change be measured?

I asked one of the pioneers in the study of forest health, Dr. Barrett Rock,
professor emeritus of the Institute for the Study of Earth, Oceans, and Space
at the University of New Hampshire. Rock, who has a PhD in the microscopy
of plants, has devoted a life of research to looking down at vast swaths of
northern forest through eyes set literally in the sky—NASA's Landsat satellites.
As it turned out, the launch of the first Landsat satellite in the early 1970s
corresponded approximately with the time frame when the climb in average
global temperature due to climate change was accelerating.

While most of us get caught up in observing the natural world in short
time frames, a temporal version of "not seeing the forest for the trees," Rock
has spent more than three decades viewing forests from a long-range planetary

perspective. His use of space-age technology to measure the health of planet Earth and monitor the seasonal changes in foliage began in the early 1980s at NASA's Jet Propulsion Lab in Pasadena, California.

Says Rock, "It's like looking through a microscope, and then stepping back 500 miles—moving from the microscope to the macroscope." Landsat satellites map and measure visible color bands in the blue, green, and red spectra. "But the longer infrared bands measured by Landsat satellites, which are not visible to the naked eye, tell us more about changes in leaf color than the visible spectrum. Physiological changes start at the end of July and early August. Shortwave infrared radiation can be used to measure the state of cellular health in trees, how much foliage is on the trees and even the amount of water in the leaves."

Satellite data is then compared with spectrometer readings taken in the laboratory to measure foliage using short- and long-wave infrared. This decades-long comparison of forest health on a large scale, combined with measurements on individual trees and leaves, has provided Rock with a unique perspective that he began to use in 1994 for measuring the response of forests to climate change. Then he dovetailed his work with national climate change assessment teams.

The Landsat 5 satellite that was launched in 1984 passed over New Hampshire every sixteen days until 2012; over nearly three decades, it recorded marked shifts in seasonal leaf coloration. "Serious change in our climate became really noticeable in the mid-1970s," says Rock, "as if a switch had been thrown at that time, including increased temperatures and reduced air quality. Significant changes in forest health also began in the 1970s and all data indicates that it is now occurring at an increasingly rapid rate. This corresponds well with what the climate change models predicted."

The first hard frosts, which bring out the most vibrant leaf colors, used to occur around the third week in September. But in recent years, these frosts have arrived later. In 2004, the first hard frost in many parts of the North Country didn't come until mid-October. As Rock has observed, "There was a time when Columbus Day was widely recognized for planning a visit to New England for spectacular colors. Now the foliar change may not have even begun by early October, and frost sometimes comes as late as early November."

Parallel findings have been reported by researchers at the University of Vermont as well as at the Harvard Forest Research Station in Petersham, Massachusetts, where researchers found that foliage now turns color an average of three to five days later than it did two decades ago. Cornell plant biologists have found that stress placed on trees due to climate change and other forms of air pollution, such as high ozone levels and acid rain, is causing many leaves to simply brown off and die without much color change. Leaves are also more prone to being invaded by fungi and bacteria seeking sugar to feed on.

Abby van den Berg, a research technician at the University of Vermont's Proctor Maple Research Center, says that fall leaf colors are initiated by shortening day length and decreasing temperature. Bright sunshine also triggers foliage coloration. "If you change the timing of the onset of cool temperatures, you alter when chlorophyll breakdown starts. Even though we have no good way to predict how climate change will affect the process that creates the colors of foliage season, it will change how the landscape will look over time."

The first frost causes the chlorophyll in leaves to start breaking down, revealing the yellow colors that had been masked by the green. A red pigment called anthocyanin is created in the autumn leaves in response to the amount of sugar found in them. The brilliant orange in sugar maples is a mix of the red and yellow pigments. Anthocyanin may help the leaves in a number of ways: protecting them from losing water during autumn dry spells, reducing frost damage, or acting as a kind of sunscreen during the bright days of autumn when leaf tissues enter a period of senescence and are particularly vulnerable to damage from sunlight.

Drought, late-season warmth, and the cloudier days that have become more common with climate change all have the effect of muting autumn leaf colors, which now often progress, as Rock has observed, "from green to pale yellow, followed by leaf fall. Stressed trees have difficulty making anti-fungal compounds, which makes it hard for them to create the beautiful bright colors."

As seen from the outermost layer of the atmosphere to the changes detected in individual leaves, the impacts of climate change on autumn foliage are striking ever closer to home. But New Englanders are accustomed to the vicissitudes of weather, and most are taking the changes in stride. Foliage season will always remain tightly woven into the fabric of the region's identity as the iconic event by which we celebrate the seasons.

# Heavy Metal Blues

IN MY YOUTH, I was an avid fisherman who listened to heavy metal music. But today's anglers catch heavy metal on a hook while singing the blues, because many of the fish commonly taken for sport and food in New England now contain toxic levels of mercury.

Most mercury released into the environment comes from coal-fired power plants, incinerators, industrial boilers, and plants that manufacture chlorine. About 60 percent of the mercury pollution that reaches the Northeast is borne on westerly winds from coal-fired power plants in the Midwest and Pennsylvania. Mercury in lesser quantities also arrives in air pollution from abroad and from regional sources.

Mercury travels through the atmosphere as a gas, as tiny, airborne particles, and as particles incorporated into rain and snow. Once elemental mercury falls to Earth, it is transformed by biochemical reactions into highly toxic methyl mercury. Methyl mercury is accumulating locally at two to four times the rate that would normally occur in nature.

Nearly half of the surface waters in the Northeast now contain levels of mercury that are above the U.S. government's threshold for safety. In some places, such as the lower Merrimack River watershed, rivers and lakes now contain levels of mercury that are significantly higher than the natural levels. Mercury "hotspots" are not confined to industrial corridors, they are also found in the waters of such rural areas as the Rangeley Lakes region of Maine, the far northern and southern waters of Lake Champlain, and the upper Connecticut River north of Barnet and Monroe.

Algae in lakes and rivers absorb mercury and are then consumed by aquatic insects, crustaceans, snails, and minnows or other small fish. These are in turn eaten by sunfish, perch, and bass. The big, carnivorous predators at the top of the finny food chain, including adult northern pike, walleye, and lake trout, hunt mostly fish and other animals. Each time a predator eats, it absorbs the mercury contained in its prey. Top predators accrue the sum of mercury that has been concentrated in their food supply. For this reason, larger predaceous fish may contain very high levels of mercury. Mercury poisoning in fish can lower the success of spawning, kill developing embryos, cause slow and abnormal growth, and even affect normal behaviors such as feeding and schooling.

Some of our most popular freshwater sport fish are contaminated with mercury, including walleye, northern pike, white perch, and lake trout. Of even greater concern for public health is that many favorite panfish, like yellow perch, brook trout, and bass, can contain high levels of mercury in polluted waters. The kinds of saltwater fish to avoid include swordfish, tilefish, shark, and king mackerel. Canned light tuna contains considerably less mercury than tuna steaks and canned albacore.

Mercury contamination creates a hardship for families who catch fish to supplement their food supply and is also a challenge for native peoples whose cultural identities and subsistence activities are inextricably linked to the traditions of fishing and hunting. When it is no longer safe to catch and eat fish from a local lake or river, yet another connection is severed between ourselves and the natural world.

The very fact that certain fish can be poisonous is ironic because, toxins aside, fish (especially salmon) contain beneficial omega-3 fatty acids that make them an excellent part of a healthy diet. This diet can ward off heart disease, slow the advance of early Alzheimer's, and decrease the chances of contracting diabetes, cancer, and depression. Pregnant women who eat safe fish in moderation may enhance the fetus's brain development, encourage good eyesight, and diminish the possibility of premature births of low weight.

*Lake trout often contain high levels of mercury.*

Eating fish that contain toxic levels of mercury, however, can damage the kidneys, liver, brain, heart, and central nervous system. This damage is most likely to occur among the fetuses, infants, and small children of mothers who ate contaminated fish while pregnant. The Food and Drug Administration and the EPA both recommend that pregnant and lactating women, infants, and young children consume limited amounts of fish and only from among the species that are safe to eat. In general, health experts recommend eating not more than two servings each week (a total of 12 ounces) of *safe fish*—meaning one of our local fish species that is less prone to high mercury concentrations and has not been caught in a mercury hotspot.

The hopeful news is that clean air laws now require that mercury emissions be contained by installing advanced air-pollution control technology during upgrades of older power plants. Michigan aims to reduce mercury released from coal-burning power plants by 90 percent within a decade. Since 1998, mercury emissions in New England and eastern Canada have been cut by more than half and levels of mercury in some lakes are slowly dropping.

As airborne emissions are curtailed, how long will it take for mercury levels to begin dropping in aquatic ecosystems? One computer modeling study of lakes in northern Wisconsin predicted that, if emissions are reduced by 5 percent, it may take nearly a decade for mercury concentrations to start declining in fish. A field study of lakes in northern Minnesota, conducted between 1998 and 2012, found that the rate at which new mercury pollution was being deposited had dropped by a third. In the waters of two lakes, mercury contamination had fallen by 46 percent, and by a third in the tissues of year-old yellow perch. Another lake showed no change in mercury levels, while a fourth lake showed a slight increase.

Recovery from airborne mercury pollution is going to take time, and will vary from place to place. If the trend holds, and mercury emissions from power plants and other sources continue to decrease, lovers of fish and fishing may be able to cast their hopes toward a brighter, though distant future.

To find out where your favorite fish (and fishing hole) fits in the larger mercury picture, visit: pubweb.epa.gov/region1/eco/mercury/newengland-fish.html.

# Fang versus Fungus

IN THE CASE OF SNAKE FUNGAL DISEASE, if the Jedi Knight from Star Wars, Obi-Wan Kenobi, had summoned the power of nature by uttering, "The spores be with you," he would have been spot on. This infectious organism features minute spores that produce a fungus capable of defeating powerful venomous snakes. Virtually unheard of in the wild prior to 2006, *Ophidiomyces ophiodiicola* has been found on snakes in nearly a dozen states, including New Hampshire, Vermont, New York, New Jersey, and Massachusetts in the Northeast, as well as Florida, Wisconsin, Ohio, Illinois, Tennessee, and Minnesota.

Snake fungal disease, or SFD, causes snakes to develop opaque eyes, scabby scales, and misshapen nodules on their heads and bodies. Their skin swells and thickens, develops ulcers, and sheds prematurely. Because SFD occurs on animals in captivity, where it thrives in warm, moist conditions, some scientists suspect that the fungus may have migrated into the wild as temperatures and humidity have increased. Climate change may also make it easier for diseases to spread during the winter, when many snakes hibernate en masse underground.

Dr. Jeffrey Lorch of the University of Wisconsin-Madison has conducted most of the recent fungus cultures on snakeskins for the U.S. Geological Survey's National Wildlife Health Center. According to Lorch, "Anecdotal field reports from herpetologists and field biologists suggest that SFD may have occurred in North America for quite some time. *O. ophiodiicola* appears to currently be widespread in the eastern United States, and we are not aware of *O. ophiodiicola* being found in wild snakes in other parts of the world. For these reasons, it is entirely possible that *O. ophiodiicola* is native to North

America." (Lorch's previous research was instrumental in identifying the fungus that causes white-nose syndrome, which has killed millions of bats throughout the Northeast.)

SFD infects all kinds of snakes—from rat snakes to rattlers. "It is likely that most snake species in eastern North America can contract SFD," says Lorch, "but we really do not know the population-level impacts at this time or how the infection varies between species. The greatest concern has arisen with snake species that occur in small, isolated populations, for which losses of even a few animals could severely limit the ability of those populations to persist or recover. These include timber rattlesnakes in the Northeast and massasauga rattlesnakes in the Midwest." All of the massasauga rattlesnakes that were discovered infected with SFD in Illinois died, and the fungus is suspected of having wiped out half of a New Hampshire population of timber rattlesnakes between 2006 and 2007.

Timber rattlesnakes are endangered in Vermont, New Hampshire, Massachusetts, and Connecticut, and are believed to be extinct in Maine and Rhode Island. Wherever they do occur, rattlesnakes survive as relict populations that harbor little genetic diversity, so it's less likely that an individual will emerge that is resistant to SFD. Vermont's Rutland County is home to two populations

*Timber rattlesnake, Rutland County, Vermont.*

that contain the state's last few hundred individuals. In New Hampshire, rattlesnakes have been reduced to a single population.

The best way to monitor SFD is to report sightings of infected snakes to the appropriate state or federal agency. Take photographs, if you can do it safely. "Citizen reporting," says Lorch, "can help determine how widespread SFD is, which species are affected, and whether the disease poses a significant risk to snakes across the eastern U.S."

Lorch urges precautions to avoid spreading the disease, such as disinfecting equipment, clothing, and hands after handling captive and wild snakes. "It is a good idea to prevent wild and captive (particularly exotic) snakes from having any sort of contact with one another if one of the animals may be released back into the wild."

But why care if snakes disappear? Ecologists and nature writers are rarely asked, "What use are people to the environment?" But we are often obliged to justify the existence of other animals, especially those, like snakes, that are feared and maligned. As predators that slither along the middle links of the food chain, snakes keep populations of prey in check, including grasshoppers, mice, voles, rats, and other critters that frequently damage and destroy crops and gardens. Snakes provide food for larger animals, such as hawks, owls, coyotes, raccoons, and foxes. As part of the natural diversity of life, they help ecosystems to be more resilient.

Snakes also have medical uses. Ironically, snake venom is employed to culture a serum for treating poisonous snakebites. Venom is administered in measured doses to horses and sheep; the antibodies to snake venom are then derived from the animals' blood. Several drugs are based on snake-venom proteins, including eptifibatide and tirofiban, which are used to prevent blood clots in patients who are suffering minor heart attacks, or those who are having chest pains and other symptoms of an impending heart attack. When administered in time, these drugs can help prevent a full-blown infarction.

And where would humans be without these iconic animals to challenge us and serve as a force against which we take our measure? Although many people revile them, snakes and other reptiles inspire a sense of excitement, awe, and mystery. As the Hydra to our Hercules, they keep us strong and make us feel alive.

# Nesting Northward

## BIRDS ON THE MOVE

AVID BIRDWATCHERS track and respond to the movements of our feathered friends with keen interest, sometimes bordering on fanaticism. A rare species sighted outside of its normal range often leads to mass migrations among adoring fans of these avian rock stars.

But we also become concerned when we notice birds behaving in unexpected ways. Songbirds are feathered barometers—harbingers of changes in the environment. In recent years, species that normally breed in southern New England are building nests and raising broods in Vermont and New Hampshire. Although climate change is one cause, there are many other reasons.

"Some expansions of bird ranges have been taking place for a long time," says Laura Erickson, science editor at the Cornell Laboratory of Ornithology. "For instance, the increased use of bird feeders started expanding the cardinal's range north decades ago. Cardinals eat weed seeds in winter, so the limit of their winter range corresponded with where snow was deep enough to cover the weed seeds."

Although winter bird feeding has been encouraging cardinals to move north since at least the 1950s, the relatively moderate winter weather and diminishing snow cover of recent decades have also encouraged cardinals to expand their range.

Northern mockingbirds and tufted titmice are other well-known northward drifters. Erickson has observed that the nesting range of the beloved titmouse—with its outsized call of "Peter, Peter, Peter," and tiny, cardinal-like crest—is shifting north, especially in New England. "They're a bird of the

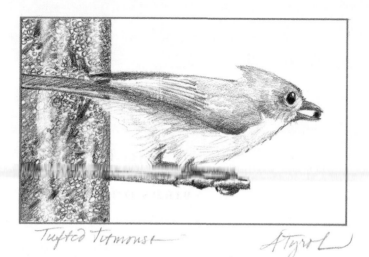

*Tufted Titmouse* *ATgirl*

beech/maple forest, so changes in forest composition to hardwood, along with more bird feeding, have contributed to their increase."

In recent years, field studies for new editions of the *Atlas of Breeding Birds* in Vermont and New Hampshire have revealed dramatic shifts of breeding ranges toward the north since 1985, when the Vermont Institute of Natural Science published the first such atlas in the United States. Trends reveal that the summer ranges of cardinals, titmice, and mockingbirds continue to grow, along with those of the purple martin, orchard oriole, cerulean warbler, blue-gray gnatcatcher, rough-winged swallow, and willow flycatcher. Red-bellied woodpeckers only began breeding in southern Vermont during the mid 1990s, but they're now breeding in many locations and are visiting bird feeders more often. This is also true of Carolina wrens.

According to Erickson, "Carolina wrens are truly a non-migratory bird. After the nesting season, an individual used to die if it scattered too far north. Their range has been expanding because temperatures are moderating and they've shown more action at bird feeders. They're also a bird of the hard-woods, and have responded to increases in hardwood forest habitat."

"Red-bellied Woodpeckers are also associated with hardwood trees," she continues. "Some of our conifers are more prone to diseases as winters become more mild, and habitat gradually changes to hardwoods."

Although our changing climate has enabled many birds to expand their ranges into northern New England, it can have an adverse impact on the birds that already live here. As the climate warms, habitat is gradually transformed. The spruce-fir forest of uplands and mountain slopes changes into hardwoods. Birch, beech, and maple forests grow into oak and hickory.

Along with these changes in habitat, some of our signature northern New England summer birds will likely decline, or disappear, including evening grosbeaks, ruffed grouse, winter wrens, red-breasted nuthatches, dark-eyed juncos, both yellow-rumped and black-throated green warblers, and even New Hampshire's state bird, the purple finch. Other, now-southern species will begin to appear, like the blue grosbeak, white-eyed vireo, summer tanager, hooded warbler, and black vulture.

The onset of a milder climate can alter the ranges of birds for other reasons, including fewer instances of extreme cold spells that can kill birds outright, and changes in the life cycles of insects and plants in response to longer growing seasons. Hotter summers tend to increase the harm caused by air and water pollution while simultaneously making our climate more favorable to a greater number of invasive plants and animals that compete with native species. Research has shown that warmer weather and increased rainfall will decrease the supply of larvae that are eaten by black-throated blue warblers. This hurts the survival of adults and the young birds they are raising.

Some adaptable birds, like the black-capped chickadee, learn to alter the timing of their nesting behavior to allow for changes in the dates of the insect hatches that normally provide food for their young. During years when springtime comes earlier than usual to the north country, however, long-distance migrants may arrive after some of the insect foods they need for raising a brood have already passed their peak. This is especially true for mi-

*Gray jay or "whiskey jack."*

grants from the tropics that overwinter in a relatively consistent climate, and so must rely on seasonal cues other than temperature and plant growth to signal migration. These birds set their internal clocks to such environmental cues as changes in day length and the onset of dry or wet seasons to tell them when to set off for their breeding grounds to the north.

Birds in extreme environments face an especially difficult struggle to adapt, like the handsome gray jay or "whiskey jack," which generally lives in high, subalpine spruce forests. As Laura Erickson explains, "Gray jays are scavengers that cache their food in the fall, such as carrion. They nest in February, but winter thaws have been spoiling their food when they most need it." Other subalpine birds—like Bicknell's thrush and the blackpoll warbler—could disappear altogether from this region.

In the coming decades, northern New England (along with the rest of the world) will witness a landmark ecological era during which avian species will adapt and survive, move on, or perish. A National Audubon report of early 2009, including more than 300 kinds of North American birds, concluded that the ranges of half of these species had moved north by at least 35 miles in the past 40 years. For birds, change may be the only constant on their horizon.

# Teenage Mutant Frogs

DURING THE SUMMER OF 1996, I led a field trip to Silver Lake State Park in Barnard, Vermont. A few parents and a gaggle of children—bedecked in flippers and water wings—lugged our gear to shore. Soon some kids came up the path toting a plastic bucket.

"Something's wrong with these frogs!"

"Yeah, some don't have any feet."

Inside the bucket squirmed scads of young green frogs missing toes, feet, or the entire lower half of one or more legs.

"That's gross!" said a budding scientist. "What happened to them?"

I explained the theories about what might cause these abnormalities, but my answer didn't satisfy because there were too many possibilities. A decade later, we have more information but an even greater number of questions.

Rick Levey, an environmental scientist with the Vermont Agency of Natural Resources, says, "Amphibians are hard to study without doing exhaustive field studies." Discerning the effects on individual species requires detailed research of each possible cause and its impacts.

Frogs truly are at one with their environment and everything it contains. Their eggs grow and develop immersed in water with no shell for protection. Frog skin is highly permeable—water, air, and anything those mediums contain can pass through it.

Northern leopard frogs and green frogs are most affected. Other local amphibian species with abnormalities include the wood frog, mink frog, bullfrog, pickerel frog, and American toad.

Mark Ferguson, a zoologist with the Vermont Fish and Wildlife Department's Nongame and Natural Heritage Program, says, "I have seen northern leopard frogs that were missing eyes and even some with extra limbs."

Researchers at the Vermont Agency of Natural Resources have collected more than 11,000 northern leopard frogs since 1996, primarily young-of-the-year froglets that hatched in early July. According to Levey, "Abnormality rates range from 0 to 10 percent. Abnormalities include truncated limbs, missing digits or no limbs at all."

A 1997 study conducted on the northern leopard frog by Middlebury College, in collaboration with a number of state and federal agencies, found that about 8 percent of the frog population had some kind of abnormal physical trait.

The many possible causes of amphibian abnormalities include pesticides, fertilizers, and increased exposure to ultraviolet radiation. In addition, parasitic worms called trematodes may damage cells in tadpoles and cause abnormal legs and extra limbs to grow, but this is not a significant cause of deformities in our region.

According to Mark Ferguson, "It's probably a combination of things compounding each other."

Depletion of the ozone layer in the upper atmosphere has increased the amount of UV-B radiation that amphibians are exposed to in recent decades. High levels of UV-B can cause abnormal growth.

*Malformed northern leopard frog.*

In environments contaminated with pesticides, the algae that tadpoles eat contain toxic substances that can build up in tissues. For example, a hormone-like substance called retinoic acid causes deformed limbs. Pesticides become concentrated in dry years as the volume of water shrinks. This, coupled with higher temperatures, leads to more deformities. Rick

Levey cautions, however, that researchers in Vermont have "never found levels of pesticides that were high enough to cause limb abnormalities."

Fertilizers washing into waterways can cause certain kinds of blue-green algae to grow, which generate toxins that have a similar effect on frogs as retinoic acid.

Pharmaceuticals and cosmetics also can disrupt normal hormone function in frogs. High concentrations of compounds from personal-care products and medicines (that we flush down the drain) may cause effeminization in frogs: males have reduced male sex organs, none at all, or begin to grow female organs. Research shows that pesticide levels one-hundredth of those needed to cause limb deformities can cause sex changes.

Not knowing the timing of an adverse impact can pose challenges when sleuthing an abnormality. In dry years, for example, when tadpoles cluster by the hundreds or thousands in their pools, predators (and even other tadpoles) may nibble on and damage the "buds" from which arms and legs grow. A month later, those young frogs may have deformed limbs.

Even if abnormal frogs survive for a time, it's hard for them to catch food and escape predators when they can't hop effectively. If abnormalities continue to increase, population levels will likely decline. "Deformed frogs may be weak going into winter because they're not as mobile and aren't feeding as well," says Levey.

Accurate, systematic records of sightings are invaluable. In the late 1980s and early 1990s, a teacher whose students studied frogs in the King's Bay area near Plattsburgh, New York, discovered that an average of 15 percent of northern leopard frogs had deformities. Following national reports about amphibian deformities in 1996, twelve calls were made to report deformities in Champlain Valley frogs. There had been only twelve to fifteen such calls in the previous seventy-five years, though this could be because few people were looking for them.

You can become a citizen scientist on the lookout for teenage mutant frogs. Keep a field notebook that tracks the details of your sightings, including date, time, place, species, and the nature of the abnormalities you discover. Then report your findings to the agency in your state that oversees fish and wildlife and enter your sightings into the FrogWatch USA database at: www. aza.org/frogwatch.

# Sugar Maples

## NOT SWEET ON CLIMATE CHANGE

UNLIKE THE ENTS in Tolkien's *Lord of the Rings*, real trees can't walk away from danger or fight their own battles. When climate becomes inhospitable, forests can only shift ranges over long periods of time. This isn't a problem when natural climate change occurs slowly. At the end of the recent post-glacial period, it took 4,300 years for the ice sheet to melt back from Middletown, Connecticut, to St. Johnsbury, Vermont—averaging 245 feet a year. Forest communities in front of the glacier gradually migrated northward in its wake.

Over a 4,000- to 5,000-year period that began about 9,000 years ago, the average temperature in the New England region was nearly 4 degrees Fahrenheit warmer than it is today, and the climate was similar to modern-day Virginia. Hemlock and white pine grew 1,300 feet higher up the mountain slopes. Evidence now clearly shows that the engines of the industrial age are taking today's climate forward into the past. U.S. Climatological Network Data reveals that the mean annual temperature has increased by 3.8 degrees since 1835, with 70 percent of this rise occurring since 1970.

Considering the two computer models used in a New England regional climate assessment study, Barry Rock, professor emeritus of the Institute for the Study of Earth, Oceans, and Space at the University of New Hampshire in Durham, predicts that "Within the next 100 years, Boston could have a climate similar to either Richmond, Virginia, or Atlanta, Georgia." These computer models project that the average regional temperature will rise between 6 and 10 degrees over the next century.

If the models prove accurate, Rock says that, "In 100 years, New England's cooler regions will no longer promote the growth of sugar maples, which are well adapted to the region's current climate. This climate will support species that now grow to the south and in lower elevations, especially oaks and southern pines. On average, trees can only move their range from 10 to 25 kilometers over a 100-year period, and the current rate of climate change will not allow enough time for trees to 'migrate' northward in a smooth transition." Under this scenario, the optimal range for sugar maples in New England could be limited to the high mountain slopes and to northern Maine. (The sugar maple's current range extends as far south as Virginia and Tennessee, though only in the higher mountains.)

David Kittredge, a professor of natural resource conservation at the University of Massachusetts and forest policy analyst at the Harvard Forest, sees several scenarios. "If we get a climate more like that of Pennsylvania, Maryland, or West Virginia, we could still have a sugar maple component in our forests." Of the five computer models created by the U.S. Forest Service to predict the geographic shift in the ranges of forest species, only one foretells that global warming will cause sugar maples to disappear completely from parts of New England. Even if the climate warms considerably, our forests will still support the growth of some sugar maples, especially in higher terrains.

Although the range of sugar maples changes slowly, the flow of sap in a sugarbush is dynamic and depends on fine temperature variations that occur daily throughout late winter and early spring. Sap flows best when nighttime temperatures drop into the mid-20s and when daytime highs reach around 38 to 40 degrees Fahrenheit.

From here the effects of climate change on sap flow are harder to predict. If the daily cycling between freeze and thaw occurs less frequently, maple sugaring will suffer, as it will if the season is shortened by several weeks. But if sugaring as we now know it is simply shifted earlier into the year, the effect could be less pronounced. Making predictions about sugaring season has always been an uncertain but popular pastime, even before the dawn of climate change.

The maple sugar industry can compensate somewhat for the uncertainties of the shifting climate. According to Dr. Timothy Perkins, director of the University of Vermont's Proctor Maple Research Center, "The best equipment in the sugar house isn't going to make you any more money. It's how you manage the sugarbush that counts." Producers need to tap their trees earlier, before the sap starts to flow, so they can gather the best quality sap of the season. Old tubing must be replaced with new, which is made of superior material and is more efficient. Getting rid of leaks in the system will help, as well as using a vacuum system for collecting sap. Collectively, these steps can help mitigate the problem.

No matter what steps are taken, the wheels have been set in motion. The question is: How far down the road—or up the slopes—will sugar maples have to travel before we put the brakes on climate change?

To view maps that predict shifts in the ranges of tree species and bird species that will be brought on by global warming, visit: www.fs.fed.us/nrs/atlas/.

STEWARDSHIP

# The Beetle and the Paparazzi

BACK IN 1986, the cobblestone tiger beetle had it all. In March of that year, the half-inch-long beetle was elected the Plainfield Town Insect, appeared on posters and T-shirts, and even became a hot topic in the national media. Reporters and photographers who descended on the New Hampshire town to cover the rare beetle's story had no idea that they were doggedly pursuing their own namesake: "paparazzi" comes from the Italian word for a kind of buzzing insect.

The island in the Connecticut River where the cobblestone tiger beetle (*Cicindela marginipennis*) lives is one of only a dozen or so such places in a few select rivers in the East, including habitats in Maine, Vermont, New Hampshire, Massachusetts, and New York. Other populations have been discovered in the region that ranges from Indiana to Alabama and New Jersey to West Virginia. In Canada the beetle occurs only in New Brunswick and Nova Scotia.

Although the beetle is found over a broad geographic area, most populations are tenuous communities of fewer than 100 individuals. Officially, the beetle is listed as endangered in Massachusetts and threatened in Vermont and New Hampshire. In Canada the cobblestone tiger beetle is listed as endangered; internationally, it is on the International Union for Conservation of Nature's red list of threatened species.

Akin to many tiger beetles, cobblestones shine with a famous beauty that contributes to their allure and their peril: insect hunters love to collect them. Their backs are olive green with a touch of bronze. Underneath they are a coppery green with a brownish-red abdomen. The upper shell has a handsome, scalloped white border.

*Cobblestone tiger beetle.*

The cobblestone tiger beetle prefers to dwell amid the cobblestones of islands and deltas in large rivers and streams, such as the Connecticut River in New Hampshire, Vermont, and northwestern Massachusetts, and the White and Winooski Rivers in Vermont. The erosive power of high waters and the grinding force of ice keep their beds of sand and cobbles free from vegetation, which is a necessary condition of their habitat.

Cobblestone tiger beetles lay their eggs from July through August. The predaceous larvae are terrestrial—living in holes in the sand and gravel that are slightly less than ¼-inch wide. Strong legs and hooks anchor them in their holes and make them nearly impossible to dislodge. Here they wait in ambush; when a fly, ant, or other prey happens by, the beetle larvae use powerful mandibles for the capture.

As tiger beetle larvae grow, they pass through several stages called instars. There are two particular life-cycle patterns among tiger beetles, based on the time of year when adults are active: "summer" species and "fall-spring" species. Depending on the species, individuals may overwinter as larvae or adults. In some cases the entire life cycle takes two years. Adults scavenge for dead food or hunt and consume live prey. Anything that isn't larger than the beetles themselves is fair game, including many insects that are harmful to crops.

Like the rest of us northerners, cobblestone tiger beetles endure brutal winters and the extreme conditions of spring thaw. The melting warmth of springtime brings "ice out"—a cataclysmic event when the river opens up and large chunks of ice grind into the riverbanks, often disturbing their habitat. During periods of high water, both beetle larvae and habitat sometimes become submerged.

Come summer, when the water level drops and exposes beds of cobbles in the river channel, the beetles bask in the heat of the sun. Alan Graham, Vermont's state entomologist and an avid photographer of all things six-legged, has a passion for tiger beetles. Graham has noticed that cobblestone tiger beetles tend to come out on sunny days. They regulate their temperature by making use of the varied environment of the cobblestones, crawling in and out of the spots of sun and shade. Sometimes they raise themselves up high on their legs to put space between their bodies and hot rocks.

Habitat loss and unpredictable water levels are two reasons that the cobblestone tiger beetle is now threatened. Large dams on rivers create deep, slow-flowing stretches of water that flood long expanses of potential beetle habitat above the dam, while periodically raising and lowering water levels both above and below the dam. Another species of tiger beetle called the "Puritan" (*Cicindela puritana*), which once lived in the Connecticut River near Charlestown, New Hampshire, has disappeared from this region.

The overall status of the cobblestone tiger beetle remains a mystery. "There are more locations than we knew of twenty years ago," says Mark Ferguson, a zoologist with the Vermont Department of Fish and Wildlife. "In 1995, new locations were found along the White River, and several have been found in other places."

"Money is limited for monitoring invertebrates," Ferguson laments. "Monitoring is hard to do with some species, because you need to go back for many years to get data and look at the long-term trend."

When asked about beetle populations, Ferguson replies, "At one of the isolated spots over the last few years, it seems to be maintaining good numbers. But more monitoring is needed for Connecticut River populations."

I recently contacted Nancy Mogielnicki, who, along with husband Peter, formed the 1980s Plainfield team that brought the tiger beetle to the fore. When asked what has happened in the intervening years, Mogielnicki replied, "Not much." Following its fifteen minutes of fame, the cobblestone tiger beetle has quietly continued to pursue its passions: stalking prey and reproducing. So far, and seemingly without assistance from people, this tenacious insect has proven a real survivor.

# Right of Passage
# for Migratory Fish

MIGRATION OFTEN EVOKES IMAGES of hawks and vultures soaring southward on rising thermals, or of V-shaped flocks of Canada geese winging to warmer climes. Birds are one of the great spectacles of nature by which we measure the passing of the seasons.

Another, hidden migratory passage happens in the quiet depths of our major waterways, those liquid skies through which fish move largely unseen, urged on by a single-minded instinct to spawn, a timeless force that drives them relentlessly on.

There was a time in the waters known by the Abenaki peoples as *Kwenitegok*, "Long River," when migratory fish moved in such multitudes that their backs appeared as a living bridge from shore to shore. After the most recent glacier melted, shad and alewives returned to migrate up our rivers for the past 10,000 years, and salmon for some 8,000 years. But free passage in the Connecticut River ended in 1798, when the first major dam was built near Turners Falls, Massachusetts. Thirteen dams eventually blocked the river's main channel— including those in Holyoke, Vernon, and Bellows Falls—sealing the fate of the great fish runs.

It wasn't until 1980, when a fish passage was constructed at Turners Falls, and later at the other dams, that migrating fish trickled back to some of their former spawning grounds. In 1992, 720,000 American shad passed the Holyoke dam—impressive but still a fraction of the historic numbers.

Not every impediment to fish passage, however, is built of concrete and stone. Migratory fish are highly responsive to temperature. American shad,

# American Shad

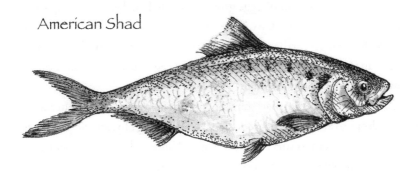

which can grow to be 2 feet long and weigh 5 pounds, spawn from May through July. Shad migrate upriver to spawn in water ranging from 41 to 73 degrees Fahrenheit. In the Connecticut River, however, they tend to stop migrating upstream once the water exceeds 68 degrees. Peak spawning occurs from 57 to 70 degrees. About half of the shad that survive spawning return to the sea, and some return two or three times during their lives.

Between 1978 and 1992, the Vermont Yankee nuclear power plant in Vernon received permits for discharging warm water into the Connecticut River, allowing for an increase in the river temperature by up to 5 degrees between mid-May and mid-October, and 13 degrees from October to May. A 2003 permit added another degree to the upper limit. During peak operation, Vermont Yankee released more than half a billion gallons of water daily. This water sometimes measured 105 degrees Fahrenheit as it entered the river, creating a heated plume that reached 55 miles downstream to Holyoke. Add to the impacts of thermal discharge the overfishing of shad in the mid-Atlantic and predation from a growing population of striped bass, and by 2005 the average annual run of shad passing the Holyoke dam had dropped by 80 percent to 143,000.

Warm water drains the energy reserves shad need to spawn and swim back to the sea. Ken Cox, fisheries biologist with the Vermont Agency of Natural Resources (ANR), says that water temperature affects migratory fish at all stages of life. "Fish migrating upriver are racing against time, against increasing temperature and date, so the window of opportunity is shrinking all the time. Artificial discharges shrink the window all the more."

"The rate of maturation of eggs growing inside females is also impacted by water temperature," says Cox. "The cooler the water, the slower the eggs mature, so fish can get further upriver before spawning. A warm slug of water can cause an increase in the maturation rate and eggs will mature lower down the river than they would normally."

In late summer, juvenile shad start moving downriver when the water temperature drops to around 65 degrees, slowly undergoing physiological changes that will enable them to survive in saltwater. Abnormal water temperatures can affect their physiology such that they won't migrate out of the river in a timely way. Cox observes that, "Warm water can delay their migration to such an extent that they may be trapped until they move downstream when water is cold enough that it may increase mortality."

When studying the impacts of warm water on migrating shad, ANR worked with an advisory committee from New Hampshire, Massachusetts, and the U.S. Fish and Wildlife Service. Says Cox, "Based on literature and our observations, we concluded that there was ample reason to be suspicious that there may be thermal impacts negatively impacting shad in the upper Connecticut River."

David Deen, river steward for the Connecticut River Watershed Council, can recall serving as a guide for fisherman in the early 1980s—a time when prime shad could still be caught in the vicinity of the Bellows Falls dam. "For people who caught their first shad on a fly rod, it was the trip of the year. But I had to give that up over the last six to seven years I was guiding because there were no fish. Those that got to Bellows Falls had to first get past Vernon and the Vermont Yankee discharge, and that, in my considered opinion, is what stopped that great shad fishery."

On December 31, 2014, Vermont Yankee ceased producing power and discharging high volumes of heated water into the Connecticut River. In 2015 nearly 40,000 shad passed above the Vernon Dam.

But the dams themselves continue to impede fish passage. In 2015 only 14 percent of the shad that passed the Holyoke dam made it above the Turners Falls dam. Until mechanisms are devised that enable healthy numbers of migratory fish to navigate past these longstanding barriers, the journeys of these intrepid piscines will be dammed.

# Days of the Living Un-Dammed

SOMETIMES, when I peer over the riverbank at a limpid pool that rests above a dam, I imagine the water as a caged animal whose energy and instincts lie in wait for liberation. At some future moment the dam will burst and, with the joy of freedom, water will rush downstream and raise the roar of a liquid tiger whose cage has been thrown open. The water's explosive energy will crash and swirl, eddy and rip downstream in an anarchic maelstrom. In time, the steady flow of a river freed will once again course between banks, reborn with the promise of experiencing the ebbs and flows of the seasons, of swelling with the abundance of a cloudburst or trickling through sun-blanched cobbles during the height of a summer drought, free once again to mirror the conditions in the land that surrounds it, and the face of the sky above.

Beyond this idyllic daydream of setting a river free, there are many consequences to removing a dam, ranging from impacts on aesthetics, history, and recreation, to the possible reduction of hydropower (a non-fossil-fuel source of energy) and changes in property values. The ecological repercussions of removing a dam are far-reaching and profound.

There are more than 75,000 dams in the United States that are at least 6 feet high. The migrating fish of New England's rivers and streams must surmount nearly 13,000 dams along their courses. Most of these dams were originally built from the late 1700s through the 1800s in order to supply water power for gristmills and sawmills, to provide for recreation and, later, to generate hydroelectric energy. As a consequence of this long history of water-powered industry, New England has more dams per square mile than any other region of the country.

Throughout New England, landowners, state officials, power companies, environmental groups, and regulatory agencies are discussing the benefits of removing old dams and restoring rivers to their historical banks. Many of these dams are small, though some straddled major rivers, like Hinsdale's McGoldrick Dam, which was removed from New Hampshire's Ashuelot River in 2001, and the nearby Winchester dam, which was removed in 2003.

Dams transform river environments into ponds or lakes—still waters that form layers with different levels of temperature, clarity, and oxygen content. Floating-leaved plants, like water lilies and pondweed, grow in the shallows, with arrowhead and cattails near the shore. During the growing season the surface layer becomes warmer than the deeper water and usually supports the growth of still-water plants like blue-green algae.

I spent much of my youth angling these environments for sunfish, perch, pike, and trophy largemouth bass, and I am still fond of the limpid idylls of historic millponds where dragonflies patrol their invisible territories, ducklings follow their mother as she weaves among the pads of sweet-scented water lilies, and yellow warblers sing their constant refrain, *Sweet, sweet, sweet, I'm so sweet!* But many of our old dams have outlived their original purposes, may be too expensive to repair, and may no longer be safe or even wanted by their owners.

*Removing a dam frees a river's flow, opens fish passage, and improves habitat.*

What happens when a dam is removed? Most dramatically, removing a dam physically re-opens a river to migratory fish, including American shad, Atlantic salmon, and blueback herring. Fish can once again navigate upstream and are no longer injured moving downstream as they pass through the turbine blades of hydroelectric plants.

Eliminating a dam also tends to cool a river's temperature, favoring the many species of fish that require consistently cool water in order to migrate. This is critical because warm water signals to many migratory fish that the spawning season is over. Even where dams are equipped with fish ladders, unnaturally warm water above the dam can create a thermal barrier that triggers an end to migration and spawning behavior in American shad and other species. (See "Right of Passage for Migratory Fish.")

In the absence of a dam, water tumbles and mixes over rocks and riffles, which balances the temperature from top to bottom and blends in oxygen. Water flushes through the minute spaces in gravel bottoms, providing oxygen and nutrients while removing wastes. The kinds of insects that thrive in free-flowing rivers return: stoneflies, water pennies, fishflies or dobsonflies (hellgrammites), black flies, and certain mayflies, crane flies, and caddisflies. Shade from overhanging trees and shrubs keeps water cool, enabling it to hold more of the dissolved oxygen that is so essential for species such as trout and alewives.

Spring floods can once again scour the river to maintain gravel, cobble, and rocky bottoms, carrying nutrient-rich sediment downstream and depositing it along the floodplain and at the mouth of the river. Some species—like the endangered cobblestone tiger beetle of the Connecticut River—require the scouring action of springtime flows to maintain critical habitat.

The free flow of water reestablishes the process of nutrient production and recycling. With natural flow, the algae that grow on rocks in riffles, along with fallen leaves, provide most of the energy that feeds the ecosystem. This organic material eventually settles out and decomposes in quiet pools. A cycle of production and decomposition occurs repeatedly along the course of a free-ranging river, forming what I envision as a *nutrient spiral* moving downstream.

Removing a dam also restores water flow to the historic river channel and reestablishes interconnections between the river and the riparian habitat along

the shore. Riparian wetlands and other habitats bordering naturally flowing rivers are more varied and changeable than those surrounding a reservoir or mill pond. Gradually, other plants and animals of the open river return and the ecological community harbors a growing diversity of species.

Dam removal does pose risks, however, such as opening the upper reaches of a river to invasive species, where newly exposed shorelines provide fertile and available habitat. (Planting native species helps to stabilize the riverbank and gives these desirable plants a chance to become established before invasives can get a toehold.) Dams also impede the upstream migration of exotic species like rusty crayfish and brown trout.

During the breaching itself, the impounded water needs to be released slowly to mitigate downstream flooding and riverbank erosion. In addition, the silt behind old dams can contain toxic sediment left over from our industrial heritage, and this silt may need to be dredged or captured with filters to reduce the possibility of poisoning habitat downstream. Finally, dams must be removed at times of year that minimize the effect on migratory and spawning fish.

In September 2013, the Dufresne Dam was removed from the Batten Kill, a tributary of the Hudson River that flows through southwestern Vermont and eastern New York. This was the only dam blocking the Vermont section of one of New England's celebrated trout-fishing rivers. The Continental Dam (a hydroelectric facility) in Easton, New York, is the last remaining dam along the main channel.

Coincidentally, while the Batten Kill was being freed, crews were demolishing the Veazie Dam along Maine's Penobscot River, opening up the channel to fish for the first time since 1913. Atlantic salmon and other ocean-going migratory fish can now swim as far as the Milford Dam, some 10 miles upstream.

In 2002, a highly successful effort began to improve passage for the spring runs of river herring in Massachusetts. Several dams and other impediments to fish passage were removed from Town Brook, a stream that empties into Cape Cod Bay just south of Plymouth Rock. Alterations were also made to existing fishways to improve access to prime spawning habitat in a 269-acre pond called Billington Sea, just 1.5 miles from the mouth of Town Brook.

But many dams persist. The Peterson Dam along the Lamoille River in Milton, Vermont, has survived a long, on-again-off-again process of removal. Taking down the Peterson Dam could restore the Lamoille's migratory runs of sturgeon, walleye, and landlocked salmon. But concerns about the cost of removal, and the loss of hydroelectric energy generation, have stalled the project.

During the past century, some 1,150 dams have been removed across the United States. Done carefully, the long-term benefits to aquatic ecosystems that accrue from removing dams outweigh the short-term disruptions of the removal process, especially when the dam in question is no longer being used for its intended purpose. Like the migratory fish that have been bumping up against these dams since they were built, however, the journey back to a free-flowing river is not always a matter of course.

# New Day for Nighthawks?

BACK IN THE MID-1980S I did all of my writing for *Keepers of the Earth* while seated at a carrel in the reclusive stacks on the seventh floor of Dartmouth College's Baker Library. If a particularly fertile run of creativity took me deep into the evening hours, I savored a late walk around the library. Overhead, swirling about the illuminated clock tower, was an aerial carousel of insectivorous birds known as common nighthawks. In and out of the bright lights they dipped and veered to catch insects on the wing while uttering an occasional "peent." It was the kind of mesmerizing display that only a languid summer night can deliver.

The sight was made sweeter because I was aware that each of those "mosquito hawks" was capable of eating more than 500 mosquitoes in a single night. Found throughout most of North America, the common nighthawk is an insectivorous machine. Flying ants are also on the menu, comprising up to one-quarter of their food. (Biologists once dissected a nighthawk with 2,175 ants in its stomach.) Beetles are their next-most-popular prey, along with grasshoppers, locusts, woodborers, sawyers, plant lice, leaf chafers, and weevils.

Even though nighthawks appear similar enough to their immediate cousin, the whip-poor-will or will-o'-the-wisp, to have fooled early ornithologists, the traditional Abenaki peoples of northern New England have always recognized the two species. The Abenaki word for nighthawk is *peskw,* by which they distinguish it from its close relative, the Eastern whip-poor-will, whose onomatopoetic Abenaki name is *pa-po-LES.* Each springtime the nighthawks' booming displays were considered a sign that the shad had begun to migrate up the Connecticut River. Early colonists, however, confused the nighthawk with the European nightjar or goatsucker, so named for its rumored predi-

lection for sneaking into the barns of the
English and Scottish countryside to suck
milk from goats.

Once fairly common in New England,
nighthawks are now seldom seen here during
the breeding season. They do, however, still
migrate through the region in healthy numbers, presumably to breed in the burns, balds, and
other clearings amid the boreal forests to the north.

In the early 1990s, during the breeding season,
New Hampshire Audubon volunteers recorded seeing
more than 100 nighthawks plying the crepuscular skies above
sixteen towns, including Berlin, Claremont, Concord, Franklin,
Keene, Manchester, and Newport. By 2021, nighthawks were only found
nesting in Concord, Keene, Conway, and likely the Ossipee Pine Barrens.
In field studies for the 2013 edition of *The Second Atlas of Breeding Birds of
Vermont*, nesting of the common nighthawk was unconfirmed, even though
their nests had been observed from 1977 to 1981.

New England is not alone. According to the North American Breeding
Bird Survey, populations of the common nighthawk declined by nearly 60
percent between 1966 and 2010—a steep decline that is being seen in many
parts of the continent. The reasons for this decline still aren't clear. Theories
include problems in the nighthawk's wintering habitat in southern South
America, or during their incredible migration flights of from 2,500 to 6,800
miles. Other possibilities include global climate change, the decline of natural
nesting habitat, and introduced species of insect that reduce the nighthawk's
native prey. The use of pesticides to control insects may have reduced food
supplies or poisoned the birds. An increase in natural predators, such as
raccoons, crows and skunks, may also be a factor.

Many biologists are concerned that nighthawks have declined from ur-
ban areas for another reason. During the past 150 years, nighthawks in our
region adapted to nesting on flat, gravel-topped roofs, in place of natural
nesting grounds, to such an extent that this became their favored nesting
location, similar to how chimney swifts have traded their natural nurseries
in old hollow trees for brick and stone chimneys. Nighthawks began nesting

on warehouse rooftops in Philadelphia as early as 1869, and on the mansard roofs of Boston in 1874. But in recent decades, nighthawks have disappeared as old gravel roofs have been supplanted with rubber membranes and other contemporary roofing materials.

It was not always so. Nighthawks naturally nested on gravel banks, rock outcrops, and beaches. They laid eggs in plowed fields and corn stubble, on tree stumps, and even on fence posts. Their penchant for nesting on bare ground following forest fires earned them the nickname, "burnt-land bird." Perhaps it was the relative safety that caused their gradual shift to nesting on gravel rooftops.

Safety does not appear to be a priority, however, during a male nighthawk's daredevil mating ritual. He plummets from the sky toward a chosen female on the ground, only to apply feather brakes and swoop up just before crashing. The resulting rush of compressed air created by his primary feathers makes a "booming" sound. (If human males had mating rituals even half as impressive, they would probably have a higher success rate than achieved by the usual line, "Haven't we met somewhere before?")

After mating, females brood two cream-colored eggs sporting granite-like flecks of color: dark brown and black to olive, gray, and lavender. Eggs are so well camouflaged that, if you ever discover a nest, don't look away or it will be difficult to find again. Females incubate the eggs, but males help feed and protect the young. When nests or chicks are threatened, nighthawks draw off intruders by feigning injury and moving from the nest. That failing, they fan their wings and tail feathers, stand their ground and hiss.

Perhaps it is because of their unique attributes, or their mysterious crepuscular flights, that nighthawks are beloved by many avian enthusiasts, who are now coming to their defense. Since beginning New Hampshire Audubon's Project Nighthawk in 2007, volunteers have created gravel nesting patches on many flat rooftops in hopes that resident nighthawks will nest. Starting first in Keene and Concord, gravel nesting patches have since been installed on rooftops in numerous towns, ranging from Concord to Hanover, and from Claremont to Woodsville. During the past decade, annual sightings have been spotty in historic sites, and only a handful of nests recorded, both on gravel rooftops and in natural nesting sites.

With so much still to learn about the enigmatic nighthawk, it may take more than experimenting with nest patches on gravel to understand how nighthawks can be returned to the skies of New England. As we have seen in recent decades with the recovery of other beloved birds—such as the bald eagle, peregrine falcon, and osprey—success requires long-term research, dedication, and hard work. Perhaps, one future day, nighthawks will again dazzle in the lights of Baker Library's clock tower and return to other historic haunts, thrilling onlookers with their sweeping acrobatics.

# When Nature Comes Knocking

Do you realize that if I didn't eat them, bugs would get so numerous,
they'd destroy the earth? Spiders are really very useful creatures.
—Charlotte, in E. B. White's *Charlotte's Web*

We two-leggeds build inviting habitats and fill them with ample food supplies. We heat these spaces in winter, cool them in summer, and keep them dry year-round. And when our wild neighbors have the audacity to move in, we frequently kill them on sight. The spider that sat down beside Little Miss Muffett, of the famous nursery rhyme, was lucky that she chose flight over might.

My wife and I recently restored an old brick farmhouse that was built in 1790, back when Vermont was still an independent republic. We removed walls and ceilings to expose and repair the original structure, then vacuumed every nook and cranny to get rid of debris left behind by two centuries of sundry inhabitants.

The cavities were crammed with butternut shells and tiny ears of corn that had been stripped clean—the work of red squirrels and mice. After we pried back a battered kickboard near the kitchen, a river of ancient wheat seeds cascaded onto the floor. These must have been pilfered from human food stores and cached by mice during an era when Vermont farmers still grew their own wheat. I saved some of those seeds to see if I can resurrect what could be a lost heirloom variety.

Most of the wall and attic spaces were stuffed with clumps of useless insulation, replete with evidence of mice: countless droppings, pee-infused nest material, rodent skeletons, and desiccated mouse-mummies. These were the remnants of nesting deer mice or white-footed mice—the most common denizens of homes in the hinterlands.

Amid the myriad nests of wasps, mud daubers, and mice, countless ancient spiderwebs festooned the roof rafters and the basement joists. For more than two centuries spiders wove their webs unseen, spinning silk as soldiers fought the Civil War, snagging their prey as Charles Lindbergh flew across the Atlantic and while the Apollo 11 astronauts walked on the moon.

The network of webbing was so extensive that I couldn't help but getting entangled. As I squeamishly tore at the strands of silk, my imagination conjured up images of the climactic scene near the end of J.R.R. Tolkien's *The Two Towers* when, deep in the shadowy subterranean passages of Torech Ungol, the giant she-spider Shelob ambushes Frodo Baggins and Samwise Gamgee on their way to Mount Doom. This archdruid of arachnids uses her thick silk to wrap up Frodo like a Hobbit hot-pocket.

Most of the webbing I encountered was spun by the common house spider, *Parasteatoda tepidariorum*—a round-bodied arachnid, about one-tenth to one-third of an inch in size, often with banded legs. This species is one of

the "cobweb" spiders, known for their messy-looking snares. It seeks warmth and shelter in the quiet corners of our homes, and earned the species name, *tepidariorum*—Latin for "warming house"—because of its propensity for living in greenhouses. When a mosquito, silverfish, or other prey is captured in these "cobb webs," sticky silk is used to reel in the hapless meal and wrap it tightly. The prey is injected with a powerful enzyme that liquefies its organs so that the spider can suck them up. Brown egg sacs each contain up to 400 eggs.

In time, I worked my way up to the top of the house. Balanced on a rooftop while painting a dormer, I inadvertently invaded the flyway of a colony of paper wasps going in and out of a soffit vent. They buzzed loudly to warn me off; sometimes a wasp landed on my face or neck and crawled around ominously. Since I had no free hand—with a paint can in one and a brush in the other—I allowed the wasps to creep around on my skin, trying to quell my nerves and exude an air of calm, all while continuing to paint.

I now do my writing in an office alcove beneath that same roof. As with many south-facing locations in old houses, this is the most active animal abode. I maintain a live mousetrap in the nearby crawl space. Some time ago, I heard skittering in the wall, followed by the sound of the trap tripping. When I checked, the trap was closed and the seeds gone, but there was no mouse inside. Over the next few weeks I tried every conceivable contrivance to catch whatever tiny creature could pull off such a trick.

Finally, I stayed up one night, tweaking the trap and re-baiting it repeatedly. Sometime after midnight, the trap clicked shut and started to rattle. I looked inside to find a masked shrew—one of the smallest mammals in the world—wiggling its tiny, tubular nose at me.

My encounter with that diminutive shrew was an epiphany; it put an end to any remaining hopes I harbored of critter-proofing a house that was more than two centuries old. After three years of trying to block every conceivable crack and hole that could serve as an entryway for mice, ladybugs, spiders, and the like, I realized that "our" house is as much an extension of the natural habitats that surround it, as it is a domesticated refuge from the wild.

# Index

Page numbers in *italics* indicate illustrations.

Cornell Lab of Ornithology, 16, 18, 51, 183–84
corpse plant. *See* Indian pipe
*Corylus americana*. *See* American hazelnut
*Corylus cornuta*. *See* beaked hazelnut
cougar. *See* mountain lion
Cox, Ken, 199–200
coyotes, 19–22, 20, 21; mountain lions, comparison with, 13, 14
crayfish, northern clearwater. *See* northern clearwater crayfish
crayfish, rusty. *See* rusty crayfish
Cromwell, Alexander, 13
*crucifer*, as species name for spring peeper, 108
cup fungi, spore dispersal by, 39
cut-leaf philodendron (*Philodendron selloum*), 35

dams: on Connecticut River, 198–200; environmental impact of, 100–101, 104, 197, 201–2; need for fish passage around, 102; removal, 202, 203–5
damselflies, 94–98; as pest control, 165. *See also* dragonflies
dandelion (*Taraxacum officinale*), 150, 151; as food, 149
deadfall trap, 154; use by Abenaki, 153
Deen, David, 100, 200
deer mouse. *See* mice
diapause: described, 55; examples, 56–57
"The Dispersion of Seeds" (Thoreau), 39
DNA, mountain lion sightings and, 14, 15

dormancy, 62–63; in ponds, 84; of spring peepers, 107–8; sugar maples and, 54; of turtles, 85
Draco, 135, 136
dragonflies, 94–98; adult emerging, 95; nymphs, 70; as pest control, 165. *See also* damselflies
dragonhunter (*Hagenius brevistylus*), 97
Dufresne Dam, 205
dulse (*Palmaria palmata*), as edible red seaweed, 159–60
dwarf wedge mussel (*Alasmidonta heterodon*), 103–6, 104

eastern white oak (*Quercus alba*), 168; acorns, 168
ebird.org, 51
ebony jewelwing (*Calopteryx maculata*), 97, 97
echolocation, 10
eels. *See* American eel
"electric light bug." *See* giant water bug
Ellingwood, Mark, 15
elm, American, 37, 121
*Elodea canadensis*. *See* Canadian waterweed
*Enallagma civile*. *See* familiar bluet
Erickson, Laura, 16, 18, 183–84, 186
Errington, Paul, 60
European nightjar, confusion with common nighthawk, 206
exotic pets, mountain lion sightings and, 15

*Fagus grandifolia*. *See* American beech
fairy smoke. *See* Indian pipe

Printed and bound by CPI Group (UK) Ltd, Croydon, CR0 4YY

13/04/2025

14656512-0002